CONTENTS

Chapter 1 Consumer Trends

Chapter 2 Shoppers' Rights

Chapter 3 Ethical Buying

OTHER TITLES IN THE ISSUES SERIES

For more on these titles, visit: www.independence.co.uk

A note on critical evaluation

Because the information reprinted here is from a number of different sources, readers should bear in mind the origin of the text and whether the source is likely to have a particular bias when presenting information (just as they would if undertaking their own research). It is hoped that, as you read about the many aspects of the issues explored in this book, you will critically evaluate the information presented. It is important that you decide whether you are being presented with facts or opinions. Does the writer give a biased or an unbiased report? If an opinion is being expressed, do you agree with the writer?

Consumerism and Ethics offers a useful starting point for those who need convenient access to information about the many issues involved. However, it is only a starting point. Following each article is a URL to the relevant organisation's website, which you may wish to visit for further information.

The consumer in 2010

Final report commissioned by The Consumer Council of Northern Ireland – summary.

⇨ The economy, uncertainties about the future and the cost of living are the biggest concerns for consumers today.

⇨ Many are worried about public spending cuts and where they are likely to hit. Health, education and policing are the areas most would like to see protected from cuts.

⇨ Consumers are adapting to their changed economic circumstances by adjusting their shopping behaviour and attitudes to money and saving. For example, many have cut down on holidays and going out and are now shopping around for best prices. However, while the recession has triggered a more cautious attitude towards spending money, credit card borrowing is on the rise.

⇨ Employment issues, the prospect of lower social benefits through future public spending cuts and higher prices brought about by the increased VAT rate are impacting on all consumers, especially the vulnerable groups in Northern Ireland. In particular, those on low household incomes, older people and young families are struggling to keep up with their finances.

⇨ Rural consumers are disadvantaged through lack of choice and access to many goods and services, with public transport, energy supply and telecommunications/Internet services being the most important ones.

⇨ Water charges are a big concern amongst consumers today with many worrying about the additional financial burden the introduction of the charges would bring. Many are also concerned about the fairness of how water charges will be introduced and implemented.

⇨ Value for money, fairness, choice, transparency and accountability are general themes that matter most to consumers. Many feel disadvantaged compared to the rest of Great Britain, for example, in terms of the cost and choice of home energy, transport and insurance.

⇨ There is a general perception that many issues are due to a lack of competition in Northern Ireland and that opening up markets would not only bring better prices and more choice for consumers but also improve other aspects, such as service quality in general.

⇨ Online technology fundamentally impacts on consumers today and is radically changing the way people inform themselves, shop and engage with suppliers and other consumers. The Internet brings better information, choice, access and value for money. However, while many benefit from this trend a digital divide is apparent with members of vulnerable groups most likely to fall behind and be excluded in today's age of the e-consumer.

24 September 2010

⇨ Information from The Consumer Council for Northern Ireland. Visit www.consumercouncil.org.uk for more.

Retail key facts

Information from the British Retail Consortium.

⇨ In 2010, UK retail sales were over £293 billion.

⇨ The retail industry employed over 2.9 million people as at the end of December 2009. This equates to 11% of the total UK workforce.

⇨ The BRC-Bond Pearce Retail Employment Monitor showed that in quarter four of 2010, retail employment was 0.6% higher than in the same quarter a year earlier, equivalent to 3,900 more jobs.

⇨ 9% of all VAT-registered businesses in the UK are retailers, with the total number currently at 188,320.

⇨ In 2010 there were 286,680 retail outlets in the UK.

⇨ More than a third of consumer spending goes through shops.

⇨ The retail sector generates 8% of the Gross Domestic Product of the UK.

⇨ Sales over the Internet account for around 8% of total retail sales, despite strong growth in recent years.

THE CONSUMER COUNCIL / BRITISH RETAIL CONSORTIUM

The problem isn't consumption – it's Consumerism

Information from Conservation Economy.

By Jon Alexander

I want to start this article by recognising an important fact. We all consume. And we always will. The act of consumption is merely the act of using something, and we will always need to use things to fulfil fundamental human needs.

> **The act of consumption is merely the act of using something, and we will always need to use things to fulfil fundamental human needs**

There is a very important difference, though, between consumption and consumerism. If consumption is the act, consumerism is the social system which exists when that act becomes defining of a society. And it's consumerism that causes the problems. Consumerism takes the act of consumption and turns it into the defining act of our role as social beings, rather than one expression of that role. We all consume, but in a healthy society, we should also participate to an equally significant extent in social groups and relationships that are beyond consumption. We should produce, and we should be citizens.

But in a Consumerist society, these other roles fade into the background. And this is dangerous, because with our roles as producers and as citizens (among others, perhaps) go balance and perspective in our societies. As Consumers, we become the centre of the universe. We have an inflated sense of our own importance. We have no real responsibility to anyone other than ourselves – we must look after our own interests first and foremost, and so become Savvy Consumers.

With consumerism, we lose our connection with where the products and services we consume come from, because we lose any real understanding that things have to be produced somewhere, by someone. But why should we question how a £4 radio or a £1 Christmas tree is produced? Why should we engage in the debate about organic food, when the FSA tells us the nutritional value is no different? The limit of our responsibility is to do the best for ourselves, by getting the quality we want at the best possible price; and to do this as often as possible in order to feed our insatiable economy.

With Consumerism, we no longer have real responsibility as citizens, because we become merely the Consumers of the political parties. Our role in representative democracy as it stands in this country today is merely to be marketed to, and if we are sufficiently wooed, to choose the best value for ourselves as individuals. We have no responsibility even to vote, and many – even most of us – do not.

With the possible exception of the United States, we in the UK are the most fundamentally (perhaps even fundamentalist) Consumerist state in the world. Look at the rhetoric of Bush and Blair in the aftermath of 9/11, directly equating consumption with the fulfilment of civic duty, the maintenance of our way of life. Look at our language; how often do you hear people described as consumers, relative to any other role? And now we have a Young Consumer of the Year Award for our children to aspire to. They work towards it in school hours. Increasingly, to be a good consumer is the future for which our schools prepare our children. Is this really what we want?

> **If consumption is the act, consumerism is the social system which exists when that act becomes defining of a society**

And what is the role of the advertising industry in all this?

To my mind, the advertising agencies are the unwitting priests of this new, emergent religion. We give the short, sharp, but intensely frequent sermons which help maintain the dominance of consumerism. Lesson one when you start at a creative agency is that the average person sees 3,000 commercial messages a day; we all know this statistic, told to us to help us understand the challenge of 'cut through'. But look at that statistic in a different light, as the number of times we preach to our faithful every day. Compare this frequency with the Koutoubia in Marrakech, which calls the city's Muslims to prayer a mere five times per day.

29 April 2010

⇨ The above information is reprinted with kind permission from Conservation Economy. Visit www.conservation-economy.org for more information on this and other related topics.

Unleashing the new consumer power

Information from Consumer Focus.

By Philip Cullum

Executive summary

It used to be said that people in Britain just meekly accepted mediocre service and poor-quality products. But change is in the air.

A new breed of more active, powerful consumers is emerging, people who are willing to throw their weight around when they need to. They are happy to work with smart businesses to help them improve and innovate. They will reward the good guys (through their spending of £873 billion a year) as well as penalising the bad guys.

The growing confidence among consumers that they can take on big business and win, increasingly isn't about action by established organisations. Rather, we've seen individual action by a new breed of 'citizen enforcers', and change being driven by instinctive consumer outrage and the desire to improve things.

Half the population now think consumers have more power to influence business. Three-quarters say they now make more of an effort to get the best deal. UK consumers are now leaving well over 100 million comments online every year.

The challenge now is to broaden and deepen this powerful shift, extending it to more markets and more people, including those who are most disadvantaged. This won't happen on its own. Consumer Focus is, with others, working to enable these conversations and open up organisations and services to greater scrutiny and innovative thinking.

This will help deliver the Government's ambition for a 'big society' of empowered consumers and communities, with people supported to help one another and make decisions for themselves.

Unleashing the new consumer power
The benefits of consumer power

Britain is stronger when the people buying and using services and products are better able to make decisions for themselves. As President John F. Kennedy[1] put it nearly 50 years ago, 'If consumers are offered inferior products, if prices are exorbitant... if the consumer is unable to choose on an informed basis, then his dollar is wasted... and the national interest suffers.'

According to Irwin Stelzer[2], 'Successful economies are ones in which consumers are sovereign.' Michael Porter[3] said in his review of UK competitiveness, 'the importance of advanced and sophisticated domestic demand grows as advanced economies progress'.

There is real strength in having an economy of active, powerful and well-informed consumers able to act on their own behalf – and support one another – in getting the best deal and highest quality. In 2009, UK consumers spent £873 billion.[4] This potentially gives them tremendous power, both individually as buyers and users of goods and services, and collectively in their wider economic impact.

The economic theory is clear. Consumer confidence, and people's decisions to spend or save, has a huge effect on the economy; consumers help to make markets work. Their sensitivity to price and quality regulates firms and promotes efficiency and improvement. Improving confidence leads, in static terms, to lower prices, but also to dynamic benefits in terms of increased innovation and economic growth.

But where things go wrong, where there is insufficient competition, consumers – particularly those who are at a disadvantage – get a raw deal and our businesses lose the sharpness that they need to succeed in export markets. Where consumers do not have the information and skills to choose the best deal, or where irresponsible business behaviour is not challenged, the worst companies prosper at the expense of the best. Where public services are run inefficiently or designed and delivered in a way that suits providers, not users, people who need those services are let down and taxpayers' hard-earned money is wasted.

As the Business Secretary Vince Cable has said, 'making this country a good place to do business' sometimes means 'arguing for more competition... [and] better protection for consumers from shady practice'.[5]

Our vision

Consumer Focus's vision for the UK economy is:

⇨ Several providers competing for consumers' business (in every market where competition is possible) on price, quality and service, driving innovation and UK competitiveness.

⇨ Consumers are willing and able to assess and compare services and products easily, identify and choose the best deal for them, and switch where it is in their interests.

⇨ Consumers are increasingly able to collaborate, learning from one another, and aggregate their buying power (sometimes on a cross-sectoral basis) to obtain the best deals and reduce detriment.

⇨ New businesses are able to enter markets easily and challenge incumbents, secure in the knowledge that

ISSUES: CONSUMERISM AND ETHICS   3   chapter one: consumer trends

large established businesses will not be allowed to create and exploit undue market dominance.

⇨ Consumers are aware of their rights and have proper access to redress when things go wrong.

⇨ Organisations encourage and learn from complaints.

⇨ Consumers are able to make well-informed sustainable choices.

⇨ Consumers at a disadvantage are given appropriate levels of assistance and protection, have access to decent and affordable essential services and do not face the double disadvantage of being expected to pay more or accept less than other people where the costs of provision do not justify this difference.

⇨ In key sectors, the right decisions about long-term investment are taken at the right time and the costs are fairly apportioned.

⇨ Where regulation is thought to be necessary to protect consumers or make markets work, the long-term consumer interest is at the heart of decision-making.

⇨ Public services are designed and run with, not just for, users, who are able to hold providers to account and contribute to taking tough decisions about priorities.

In short, we want to see a vibrant, sustainable economy that works for all, marked by innovation, accountability and responsibility.

Ten million UK adults have never used the Internet, including four million of the most excluded and disadvantaged people

Delivering this will require creative new approaches. We are encouraged by the Government's starting-point:[6]

'Our government will be a much smarter one, shunning the bureaucratic levers of the past and finding intelligent ways to encourage, support and enable people to make better choices for themselves... The Government believes that action is needed to protect consumers, particularly the most vulnerable, and to promote greater competition across the economy. We need to promote more responsible corporate and consumer behaviour through greater transparency and by harnessing the insights from behavioural economics and social psychology.'

This article explains how this approach could build on emerging trends of consumer power.

The rise in consumer power

This is a generation of more powerful, connected, collaborative consumers. There are real signs that consumer power matters more now and is stronger than ever before.

Our survey found that 50 per cent of people believe consumers have more power now to influence business standards; just 17 per cent disagree.

This is reflected in welcome signs of change in the position of consumers in the economy. Policy makers and service providers now talk far more about the consumer interest, in the public services as well as the private sector.

There is greater understanding of consumer behaviour and how best to influence it using social marketing and 'nudge' techniques.[7]

The Internet and innovations such as mobile phone commerce potentially offer consumers the benefit of reaching goods and services anywhere and at any time. Consumers are able to shop around in a way that has never previously been possible.

In our survey, 85 per cent of consumers said that the Internet makes it easier than ever to get the best deal. This isn't just the view of younger people: nine out of ten people (90 per cent) aged 55 and over agreed, more than any other age group.

This is affecting people's consumer skills and appetite for engagement. Three-quarters (75 per cent) of people tell us that they now make a greater effort to get the best deal. Six in ten (63 per cent) think that price comparison sites are influential and, according to Ofcom, a similar number (61 per cent) say they are more likely to use these sites now than they were 12 months ago.[8] Some 2.7 million people contributed their views to the last Post Office closure programme.[9]

We are seeing increasingly complex products and services, sold in more complex ways, providing the ability for businesses and public services to meet individuals' unique needs rather than taking a 'one size fits all' approach.

Problems new and old

A large minority of people are not presently able to take advantage of these trends. Ten million UK adults have never used the Internet, including four million of the most excluded and disadvantaged people.[10] According to Ofcom, 42 per cent cite lack of interest or need as the main reason, while 30 per cent say the Internet is too expensive or they lack the skills to use it.[11] One consequence is that they end up paying a premium for their essential services – on average, £560 a year more.[12]

Alongside this, people who do not have a bank account similarly face increased costs and difficulties accessing certain services and products.

But even for the majority of people who are online, greater complexity can mean consumers are put off entering

the market or make bad judgments when faced with complicated decisions.

In the energy sector, for example, the regulator Ofgem found[13] that less than one in five domestic energy consumers are 'active' and regularly seek out competing price offers and switch on the basis of a good understanding of the range of offers available. A worrying number switch in error to worse offers. Vulnerable customers in particular struggle to obtain, or even seek, the best deals.

In the current account market, just 3.3 million (seven per cent) have switched over the last two years, far behind other comparative markets. Three-quarters of consumers (75 per cent) have never even considered switching their current account provider.[14]

In the mobile phone market, BillMonitor (the only Ofcom-approved mobiles comparison website) estimates there are 82,000 tariffs and more than seven million deals overall on offer.

Half of consumers do not know whether they are charged for calling an 0800 number from their mobile. When the existence of BillMonitor was highlighted by Consumer Focus in the media, it experienced a ten-fold increase in traffic – suggesting underlying demand for someone to cut through the complexity.

Alongside this, it is not hard to find significant problems in many markets, often which have existed for years or decades. The number of rogue traders, who deliberately purport to offer something that never materialises or is of poor quality, remains stubbornly high.

Unfair and hidden terms and conditions remain common; the shadowy 'end user licence agreements' of software companies are a modern version of this old issue.

Leading financial services companies now advertise proudly that they are not on price comparison sites, claiming they have cut out the middleman. The reality is that they do not want people to compare prices.

And the same old marketing techniques to mislead consumers remain commonplace. There are deliberate attempts to manipulate 'best buy' tables and mislead consumers – this would for example appear to be the reason why mortgage arrangement fees are now three times what they were in 2003.[15] The website FancyAMortgage comments, 'In today's competitive mortgage market some financial institutions are using a combination of higher arrangement fees and lower interest rates to manipulate mortgage comparison websites' best buy tables.'[16]

'Bait pricing' remains a common tactic of leading companies in sectors such as energy, financial services and communications, with consumers lured in with great short-term deals which soon disappear and the companies relying on consumer confusion and inertia. Consumer Focus's super-complaint on the market for cash ISAs shone a spotlight on one example of a much wider practice.[17]

Many consumers remain infuriated by low standards of service provided by big companies, who claim to offer personal service but struggle to deliver this through mass market systems and cultures which have tended to prioritise economy and volume of custom over service. Companies' practice of seeking to attract new customers with special offers that are not available to existing consumers, even those who have loyally stayed with a business for many years, is a particular bugbear for many.

Notes

1 Special Message to the Congress on Protecting the Consumer Interest, 15 March 1962

2 Irwin Stelzer, 'Why Brown is wrong for No 10', *The Times*, 29 March 2005

3 Michael E Porter and Christian H M Ketels, UK Competitiveness: moving to the next stage, DTI Economics Paper no 3, May 2003

4 Office for National Statistics, National accounts: Household final consumption expenditure at current prices, updated 12 July 2010

5 Speech to Cass Business School, 3 June 2010

6 The Coalition: Our programme for government, May 2010

7 Richard H Thaler and Cass R Sunstein Nudge: Improving Decisions About Health, Wealth, and Happiness, Yale University Press, 2008

8 The Communications Market 2010, Ofcom, 2010

9 Andy Burrows and Colin Griffiths, How was it for you? Consumer Engagement in the Post Office Closure Programme, Consumer Focus, February 2010

10 Manifesto for a Networked Nation, Race Online 2012, July 2010

11 Accessing the Internet at home, Ofcom, June 2009

12 Manifesto for a Networked Nation, Race Online 2012, July 2010

13 Energy Supply Probe, Ofgem, 6 October 2008

14 Oliver Morgans, Stick or twist? An analysis of consumer behaviour in the personal current account market, Consumer Focus, forthcoming

15 Financial inclusion Centre and Consumer Focus, From Feast to Famine, April 2009

16 www.fancyamortgage.co.uk/mortgagefees/arrangement.asp

17 Consumer Focus supercomplaint on the market for cash ISAs, March 2010

October 2010

⇨ The above information is reprinted with kind permission from Consumer Focus. Visit www.consumerfocus.org.uk for more information on this and other related topics.

CONSUMER FOCUS

Spend-emic hits British men and women

Information from uSwitch.

By Lauren Pope

A spend-emic is hitting the UK: shopaholics have an average personal shopping debt of £3,353 – nearly three times the national average – and this wave of shopaholism is affecting men as well as women.

Research from uSwitch has found that while four million women are in the grips of shopaholism, the spend-emic is affecting three million men too, and they actually owe more than their female counterparts.

An addiction to shopping has often been regarded as a female affliction, but the poll revealed that while female shopaholics owe an average of £3,353, male shopaholics are saddled with higher personal shopping debts of an average £3,425 each.

Women tend to spend a larger proportion of their disposable income on shopping – an average £2,436 a year or 51% of their total disposable income – but it seems that men have more expensive tastes. The men polled said that they spend over £570 a year on designer clothing, nearly double the £300 spent by female shopaholics. Men also spend more on grooming: an average of £338 a year on skincare and cosmetics, compared to the £191 spent by women.

The poll also highlighted some worrying trends:

⇨ 23% admit that their shopping behaviour hasn't changed because of the economic climate.

⇨ 4% are shopping more to 'cheer themselves up'.

⇨ 14% of female shopaholics budget for all of their month's spending in advance.

⇨ 41% would buy an item they really wanted, even if they knew it would push them over their overdraft limit.

⇨ Over a quarter of shopaholics either lie about the cost of their shopping or simply hide it from their partner.

The way this spending is being funded is also a cause for concern:

⇨ Half of female shoppers (50%) use a combination of credit cards, store cards, overdrafts or loans to fund their shopping sprees, but amongst female shopaholics this rises to 74%.

⇨ Female shopaholics are spending a massive 19% of their income on debt repayments, compared to a national average of 8%.

⇨ Shopaholics take longer to clear their debts – seven months compared to the average five months.

⇨ 17% admit to having sneaked items onto their partner's credit card.

Ann Robinson, Director of Consumer Policy for uSwitch.com, says: 'In today's celebrity-obsessed society, any lessons learnt from the recession have been airbrushed out of the picture. Despite the financial constraints, women have carried on copying the lifestyles and shopping habits of their idols and ignoring the debt they are racking up in the process. But this spend-emic has spread and it's clear that men too have caught on to the joys and perils of shopping.

'It's time for everyone to pay serious attention to their spending habits. Short-term debt solutions may seem an efficient way to fund spending, but they can also lead to long-term debt if not managed properly. Consumers need to stay in control of their finances – it's easy in the face of feeling impoverished to let go of the spending reins altogether. By recognising that risk and not falling victim to it, consumers can feel empowered and enjoy the pleasure-rush of a new purchase, without racking up more unsecured debt. It is all gain and no pain.'

25 August 2010

⇨ The above information is reprinted with kind permission from uSwitch. Visit www.uswitch.com for more.

© uSwitch

Household spending falls for first time in ten years

UK households spent less on clothing, transport and mortgages last year [2009] than in 2008, according to new figures released today by the Office for National Statistics (ONS).

*F*amily Spending, the annual report from ONS on household expenditure in the UK, found that in 2009 the average weekly household spend was £455.00, compared with £471.00 in 2008. It is the first drop within the last ten years.

Spending was highest on transport at £58.40 per week though this fell by eight per cent on the previous year, with half (£29.30) going towards running costs.

Of the £52.20 average weekly spend on food and non-alcoholic drink, almost three-quarters (72 per cent, £37.70 per week) was purchased from large supermarket chains

Average expenditure levels in each of the next two top categories were very similar. Recreation and Culture fell slightly to £57.90 in 2009 from £60.10 in 2008, despite higher spending on items such as leisure classes, sports admissions, cinemas, theatres and concerts. Expenditure on housing, fuel and power increased to £57.30 in 2009 from £53.00 in 2008.

Expenditure on Clothing and Footwear was £20.90 per week, slightly lower than the previous year and continuing the long-term fall in this category to the lowest figures recorded under current methods. Similarly, expenditure on Household Goods and Services such as furniture and appliances also hit a long-term low, falling from £30.10 in 2008 to £27.90 in 2009.

Of the £52.20 average weekly spend on food and non-alcoholic drink, almost three-quarters (72 per cent, £37.70 per week) was purchased from large supermarket chains, a similar proportion to the previous year.

Spending on package holidays fell from £14.70 per week in 2008 to £13.20 in 2009 with £12.30 spent on package holidays abroad, £1.30 less than the previous year.

Giles Horsfield, ONS statistician and editor of the report, said:

'This is the first annual decline in average UK household spend since the current method of recording was introduced in 2001-02, with higher expenditure on some housing-related costs such as rent, electricity and gas offset by lower spending on mortgages.

'Lower spending on diesel and fuel contributed to lower expenditure on transport, but reductions were also seen on vehicle purchases and public transport.

'It's interesting to note that expenditure fell again on clothing, which took it to a record low under current methods, for the third year in a row. Spending also fell on household goods and package holidays, but held up on sports admissions, cinema, theatre and concerts.'

Overall, average household expenditure in the UK was £461.70 per week for the years 2007-09 combined. There were five regions in which expenditure over this period was higher than the UK average: expenditure was highest in London (£552.30), followed by the South East (£523.90 per week), the East (£487.70), Northern Ireland (£485.80) and the South West (£474.10). Spending was lowest among households in the North East (£387.20), Wales (£396.10) and Yorkshire and the Humber (£400.70).

Spending was highest on transport at £58.40 per week though this fell by eight per cent on the previous year, with half (£29.30) going towards running costs

London households' high spending was partly due to the housing, fuel and power category (£80.10 per week) compared with the UK national average of £54.00 per week.

Households in rural areas had higher overall expenditure (£500.00 per week) than those in urban areas (£450.20 per week). This was reflected in expenditure on transport, where spending was highest (£75.70 in rural areas and £57.00 in urban areas), and recreation and culture (£65.80 in rural areas and £56.40 in urban areas). However, expenditure on the housing, fuel and power category was slightly higher in urban areas (£54.90 per week) than in rural areas (£52.00 per week).

30 November 2010

⇨ The above information is reprinted with kind permission from the Office for National Statistics. Visit www.statistics.gov.uk for more information.

© Crown copyright

OFFICE FOR NATIONAL STATISTICS

January's fall in family spending power beats records for second month in a row

Asda Income Tracker shows cost of living continues to rise above earnings growth.

⇨ £9 a week fall in family spending power compared to the same month a year ago is the largest decline since the Income Tracker began.

⇨ It represents the 13th month of consecutive decline.

⇨ Average UK household had £174 a week of discretionary income in January 2011, 4.7 per cent lower than a year earlier.

The latest Asda Income Tracker has revealed that in January 2011, family spending power fell by £9 per week, the largest fall on record and the second record-breaking month in a row. The average family had £174 per week to spend in January, 4.7 per cent down from £183 this time last year. When the impact of bonus payments is included, family spending power also decreased by £9 over the year to January, a fall of 4.3 per cent.

The continued decline in family spending power in 2010 and into 2011 was the result of the price of essential goods and services rising faster than net income growth. Gross incomes grew by 2.4 per cent in January 2011 year-on-year, down from 2.6 per cent in December but above the lows experienced in 2009.

The rise in inflation points towards the depreciation of sterling, rising global commodity prices and the VAT rise in January 2011. With ongoing disruption to oil supplies through Egypt and vibrant demand from emerging economies, the price of crude oil put pressures on petrol costs in January. In addition, VAT rose to 20 per cent on 4 January, and earnings growth has remained sluggish. As a result, those factors which caused the Asda Income Tracker to fall in 2010 have persisted into 2011 and are likely to continue over the short term.

Transport was yet again the largest contributor to the headline rate of inflation in January, which remained the single most important element of consumer price inflation. According to the AA, the cost of unleaded petrol rose 17.8 per cent between January 2010 and January 2011.

Charles Davis, Managing Economist at Cebr comments:

'With annual consumer price index inflation double the Bank of England's target rate, while earnings growth remains modest, average households are seeing spending power sharply eroded.

'This trend is likely to continue into 2011, as inflation remains elevated and the labour market recovery lacks conviction.'

Andy Clarke, Asda president and CEO, said:

'The latest drop in household spending power reflects what we're seeing in our stores – customers making each pound count.

'We're conscious that we're now seeing year-on-year declines in disposable income that reinforce our responsibilities to shoppers – holding back inflation, keeping prices low, and being at our best in helping them deal with whatever the economy throws at them.'

25 February 2011

⇨ The above information is reprinted with kind permission from Asda. Visit www.asda.com for more information.

Empty shops are killing UK's high streets

The number of vacant shops continues to grow, threatening the future of the high street, especially in the north of England.

By Rebecca Smithers, Consumer Affairs Correspondent

The number of empty shops in Britain continues to soar, amid warnings that some high streets will never return to their pre-recession days.

Town centre vacancy rates climbed from 12% at the end of 2009 to 14.5% at the end of 2010, according to the end of year report by the Local Data Company (LDC), which says that shops and shoppers are being hit by structural changes that threaten the future of the high street.

The study has revealed a north-south divide, with 'black spots' in the north of England and the Midlands well above the national average, with a 16.5% vacancy rate, while southern regions scored below at 12.3%.

Large towns have a higher average vacancy rate (16.5%) than smaller centres (about 12%), and the situation is worse in large town and city centres in the north of England and the Midlands, where average vacancy rates are about 19%; Yorkshire and the Humber are even higher, at nearly 21%.

The number of empty shops in Britain continues to soar, amid warnings that some high streets will never return to their pre-recession days

Rates for large centres in London, the south-east, the east and the south-west are all about 14%, while Scotland has the lowest regional rate, at 12.6%. Smaller centres in the north-west have the highest rate, at more than 17%, followed by the north-east, at 15%.

The report says: 'Whichever way you look at it, fundamental structural changes are taking place in UK retail at the retailer and consumer levels. The very fact that ten years ago the majority of a multiple retailer's stores were on a high street but now are migrating from the high street into shopping centres and out-of-town shopping parks begs the question of what will fill the high street of 2020 and beyond?'

The retail sector has been hit hard by the recession. Large chains such as Woolworths, Zavvi and Borders have closed down without new tenants moving into the space. The downturn took its toll on all sectors of the retail industry, with Threshers off-licence owner First Quench calling in the administrators on its 1,200 stores and a host of furniture chains including Ilva and the Pier have folded.

Added to that, HMV is planning to shut 60 stores, and JJB Sports is trying to offload up to 95 shops as the growth in online sales takes its toll.

Liz Peace, chief executive of the British Property Federation (www.bpf.org.uk), said: 'Many high streets will never return to their pre-recession days and, given the structural nature of these changes, the challenge for local authorities is to work with businesses, including retailers and landlords, to sensibly manage this transition and to be creative in looking for new roles and uses for empty shops.'

Town centre vacancy rates climbed from 12% at the end of 2009 to 14.5% at the end of 2010

LDC's business development director, Matthew Hopkinson, said: 'The sad reality is that the number of vacant shops is increasing, with certain areas of the country severely impacted and unlikely to recover. These high streets will never revert back to what they once were and so the composition of our town centres needs to change to reflect modern shopping needs.' The British Retail Consortium agreed that the situation was worrying and is calling for a 'retail-friendly' budget next month, placing the urgent reform of the business rate system at the top of its list of priorities. It said retailers were facing a 4.6% increase in business rates in April on top of the impact of the five-yearly revaluation last year.

Tom Ironside, the BRC's director of business and regulation, said: 'High street retailing will continue to be at the heart of communities and a vital part of our overall retailing mix. The fragile state of the economy is compounding difficulties many of our town centres have been facing for some time. Economic recovery alone will not be enough to ensure they bounce back. Town centres need to be actively planned, managed and invested in. Key issues, including the costs of doing business, parking and access and crime, need to be addressed. They must be actively planned, managed and invested in.'

15 February 2011

UK consumers continue to harbour unsafe online shopping habits

Information from shopsafe.co.uk.

By Chris Bradshaw

Research from security software firm Webroot has found that consumers in the UK and from around the globe are still unable to practise safe shopping online, because of bad habits which put their personal data and privacy at risk of compromise.

More than 2,500 people from the UK, North America and Australia were questioned as part of a yearly look at the way in which consumers indulge in e-commerce.

While 55 per cent of respondents said they would be buying most presents for the festive season using the Internet, an increase of 17 per cent compared to 2009, the report concluded that many are actually operating online in a way that is less safe and secure than in the past.

48 per cent of shoppers will directly consult a major search engine when looking for presents rather than opting to use a site with which they have previously shopped.

The issue with this approach is that phishing sites and criminals attempt to exploit the search engines to get their malicious links into the higher echelons of the results and the survey found that 59 per cent of consumers trust the highest ranked links. This represents an increase of 21 per cent over last year's figures, which could make the job of cybercriminals easier.

Many consumers said that they would piggyback on a publicly available Wi-Fi network in order to buy gifts for Christmas 2010, which again puts them at risk from hacking and malware infection.

Webroot's Jeff Horne said that one out of every seven respondents to the survey had experienced fraud as a result of online shopping in the past year. 57 per cent also reported receiving spam mail which emulated a big-name brand in order to deceive consumers.

Mr Horne recommends that those who want to be assured of safe shopping online should only use sites they trust, visit them directly and look out for obvious scams.

22 November 2010

⇨ The above information is reprinted with kind permission from shopsafe.co.uk.

© *shopsafe.co.uk*

Disgruntled shoppers ditch online grocery services

By Simon Frederickson.

A survey has found that certain members of the public are not convinced that online grocery shopping is the way forward and, after trying it, have reverted to visiting the shops in person rather than buying online.

ConsumerIntelligence conducted a study in which it discovered that 27 per cent of people who have shopped online consequently chose to go back to the high street after being dissatisfied with their experience. This news has emerged despite the fact that the number of people enjoying safe shopping online has consistently risen and the UK is one of the world leaders in this area.

Interestingly, brand loyalty is not a factor when many buy grocery products online, according to the survey. Instead it is service quality, costs and the availability of products which dictates whether or not consumers will return.

The interactive, tactile nature of shopping in store is seen as one of the main reasons that grocery shopping on the high street is preferred by some people over safe shopping online. The schemes by which online retailers substitute unavailable groceries for an equivalent product and potentially mismatch items or fail to meet consumer standards are another bugbear for customers.

Around 32 per cent of people who buy groceries online shop via Tesco's e-commerce site, while Asda is in second place with 30 per cent and Sainsbury's sits in third with 25 per cent. Despite the fact that Waitrose holds the highest customer satisfaction it still has a smaller 22 per cent stake in the market.

ConsumerIntelligence's Ian Hughes, said that supermarkets who offer online shopping to customers need to address the concerns raised by this survey. The cost of delivery and inadequate substitution techniques are sending people back to the high street, according to Mr Hughes.

© *shopsafe.co.uk*

Consumers see little difference between national and store brands

Majority of global consumers equate store brands with national brands on essential brand attributes.

Consumers from around the world feel strongly that store brands are the same as, or better than, national brands at providing a variety of benefits. This is the latest finding from a study conducted by Ipsos Marketing, *Consumer Goods*.

While store brands have built their foundation on distinguishing themselves as a good value in terms of low cost, the study suggests that consumers believe store brands provide much more than that. At least 80% of global consumers indicated that store brands are the same as or better than national brands on many dimensions, most notably meeting their needs, offering convenience, being good for their families, caring about the environment and exuding trust.

'Our data indicates that store brands are challenging national brands on a number of key brand attributes,' says Gill Aitchison, President, Ipsos Marketing, Global Shopper & Retail Research. 'In essence, the brand experience associated with store brands is matching the brand experience associated with national brands – and that is very alarming for national consumer packaged goods marketers.'

The study further indicates that global consumers are confident that store brands perform just as well as national brands: 81% say that store brands offer food products that taste as good and home products that work as well as national brands. The notion that store brands offer a sub-optimal product experience – the trade-off for lower price – seems to be fading in consumers' minds.

'Store brands are flourishing as a result of product quality improvements in conjunction with the effects of the poor economy on consumers, which has elevated purchasing of store brands,' Aitchison adds. 'The level of trust in store brands across many different product areas at a time of distrust in other sectors like banking may mean that shoppers may be less likely to return to more expensive brands in the future unless the benefits really outweigh the cost – and these will tend to be emotional benefits rather than functional benefits.'

On which benefits should national brands focus? According to Aitchison, 'The data from our survey suggests that national brands' greatest strengths vs. store brands are packaging, innovation, uniqueness and quality.

'These are important facets of the brand experience, and ones that manufacturers should consider in their brand strategy.'

These are the findings from a study conducted by Ipsos Marketing, *Consumer Goods*, via the Ipsos Global @dvisor International Omnibus, an online survey of citizens around the world. Interviews were carried out between 4 November 2009 and 13 January 2010. For this survey an international sample of 21,623 adults aged 18+ were interviewed in a total of 23 countries. The countries included Argentina, Australia, Belgium, Brazil, Canada, China, France, Germany, Hungary, India, Italy, Japan, Mexico, Poland, Russia, South Korea, Spain, Sweden, the Czech Republic, the Netherlands, Great Britain, the United States and Turkey.

29 March 2010

⇨ Information from Ipsos MORI. Visit www.ipsos.com for more information.

© Ipsos MORI

Consumer perceptions toward store brands vs national brands
Percentage saying store brands are the same as or better than national brands

Attribute	%
Providing a good value for the money	89%
Offering products that meet my needs	87%
Offering convenient products	87%
Offering products that are good for the family	86%
Offering products my family requests	83%
Offering environmentally-friendly products	82%
Offering food products that taste good	81%
Offering home products that work well	81%
Offering products I trust	80%
Offering high-quality products	73%
Offering unique products	69%
Offering innovative products	69%
Having appealing packaging	65%

Source: Ipsos MORI, March 2010

Chapter 2

SHOPPERS' RIGHTS

Know your consumer rights

Just because you have shopped around to get goods at the best possible price, it doesn't mean you don't have the same rights as any other consumer, explains Teena Lyons.

If things go wrong, you must complain. If you know what you are talking about, you can take on the toughest of blue chip companies to get satisfaction.

Step one: Act fast. The amount of time you have to complain does vary. Ideally, you should complain within a week – although some big ticket items such as a car may take longer than other simpler products such as, say, a kettle, to reveal their faults.

The key is to highlight the problem within a 'reasonable time'. The legal position is that, where the goods are faulty, if you return them within six months the shop must prove they WERE NOT faulty when you bought them. After that time, you must prove they WERE faulty when you bought them.

If you leave it too long and you might lose your right to a full refund, even if the goods were faulty. However, you may still be entitled to a replacement, reduction, or a credit note.

Step two: Don't be fobbed off. Your agreement is with the retailer, not the manufacturer. It is not up to you to chase the maker of the goods.

According to the Sale of Goods Act, 1979, the goods should be of 'satisfactory quality' and 'fit for purpose'. That means that if you bought, say, a new printer for your computer, it should not only print documents to a good quality, but also specifically carry out any purpose you required. So, if you asked 'will it be compatible with my Apple Mac computer?' and were told yes, but it won't work, then it wasn't fit for the purpose intended.

Step three: Plastic Fantastic. You have more rights if you spend on a credit card, than you do with a debit card, cash or cheque.

Under Section 75 of the Consumer Credit Act 1974, if you pay for goods worth more than £100, even partially, on a credit card then the credit card company is equally liable with the retailer.

So, if you have a problem such as non-delivery, then you can go straight to the credit card company rather than the retailer. This is very useful in cases where the retailer has gone bust, or is being obstructive.

But this is not a licence to pile everything onto credit cards because it will cost a fortune in interest. This works best for those who regularly pay off their balances, so they can get the benefit of extra rights at no cost.

Step four: Surf easy. Remember, if you are buying goods online from a UK-based company, it is just the same as buying in a shop. Plus, under distance selling regulations, you have seven working days to cancel after you get the goods, although this does not apply to fresh food or flowers. Once again, use your credit card if you want extra protection.

Written by Teena Lyons. The opinions in this article are the author's own and for general information only. Always seek independent financial advice.

⇨ The above information is reprinted with kind permission from Saga. Visit their website at www.saga.co.uk for more information on this and other related topics.

© Saga

SAGA

Online shoppers 'unaware of consumer rights'

OFT report highlights increasing number of online retailers not complying with legislation, and many consumers unaware of their rights.

By Rebecca Smithers, Consumer Affairs Correspondent

British consumers are the most enthusiastic online shoppers in Europe, but one in four worries more about shopping this way than through traditional offline outlets, according to latest research. And their fears may be justified, as despite a raft of legislation to protect consumers only one in five retailers is fully compliant.

The research by the Office of Fair Trading is designed to highlight the importance of its long-term strategy to protect consumers and make sure they are aware of their legal rights when things go wrong online.

The strategy says online shopping, worth about £50 billion a year, is key to driving innovation and competition and has delivered huge financial and practical benefits for consumers. But it warns that continuing online innovation must be met with tough enforcement to tackle new and complex forms of unfair trading that could harm both consumers and markets.

With average savings per household of £560 a year from shopping and paying bills online, and with about 40% of the UK population not carrying out any online transactions (rising to 56% among lower socio-economic groups), the OFT says consumers could be missing out on significant benefits.

Yet the OFT found that only one in five firms are fully complying with consumer law for online shopping, with the most common breaches including unfair restrictions on cancellations of orders for products. It recommends that trading standards officers work more closely with enforcement agencies and the police to swap data about errant traders.

The research also found that one in seven consumers had experienced a problem shopping online, of whom 37% were reluctant to buy online again. Two-thirds of Internet users were worried about other people accessing their personal details on the Internet.

The OFT's strategy was developed in response to issues in the *Consumer white paper*, published in July last year. The OFT said: 'Consumers don't always know their online rights or where to go to for help. The consumer landscape is fragmented with consumer organisations conveying a variety of messages regarding Internet safety, and access for consumers to redress and learning can often be limited.'

Significantly, it added, consumers are less likely to know and therefore less likely to enforce their consumer rights when buying online.

Earlier this year, the Department for Business, Innovation and Skills carried out a survey as part of the Know Your Rights campaign, which showed that three-quarters of UK consumers didn't know there were differences between online and offline consumer rights. It also showed more than one in ten consumers admit to being unsure of their consumer rights with online purchases.

According to the government's *Attitudes to Online Markets* survey, 80% of Internet users knew it was possible to claim their money back from a credit card company if the goods or services are not delivered. However, 35% were unaware they would be entitled to a refund if an item they purchased online was not delivered by the agreed date, or within 30 days of the initial order. Meanwhile, 24% of Internet users were unaware of the seven-day cooling-off period for most online purchases.

Your online rights

If you have bought online from a UK-based company, many of your rights are the same as when you buy from a shop. You also have additional rights:

⇨ Online retailers must supply clear information about the goods or services offered before you buy.

⇨ They must also provide written confirmation of this information after you have made your purchase.

⇨ A seven working-day cooling-off period during which an order can be cancelled without any reason and a full refund made.

⇨ A full refund if the goods or services are not provided by the date you agreed. If you didn't agree a date then you are entitled to a refund if the goods or services are not provided within 30 days.

These rights apply to all forms of home shopping, not just Internet sales. Although there are cases where these additional rights do not apply, including online auctions. Auctioneers, unlike other sellers, can refuse to accept responsibility for the quality of the goods they auction.

Read the conditions of sale with care. Unless the seller is a private individual, the standard terms of the contract set out in *The Unfair Terms In Consumer Contracts Regulations 1999* still apply.

10 December 2010

THE GUARDIAN

Don't keep me hanging on a customer service line

Information from Which?

By Hannah Jolliffe, Conversation Editor

Endless rounds of questions, followed by a message that 'we're experiencing a high number of calls and you might like to call back later'. Not the kind of service we want, but sadly the type we've come to expect.

Calling customer support is like a game of chance. Press one if you're considering leaving us. Press two if you're moving home. Press three if you'd like to discuss the different products we can offer you.

I'm often left a little stumped by the fact that all these options could apply to my call, so in haste I pick one at random. Then it's on to another round of options, and then another, followed by a long wait to insipid music.

And yet, when my call is finally answered, I still feel compelled to apologetically explain that I might've come through to the wrong department.

... PRESS **32** TO ALMOST GET TO SPEAK TO ONE OF OUR OPERATORS YOUR CALL IS IMPORTANT TO US .. ....

zzzzzz

Hold on a minute – or eight

We've researched this subject a few times in recent years and found it's quite normal for people to take longer than they'd like to get through to an actual person.

In 2008 we called customer helplines at broadband and utility companies and government agencies to find out how long callers had to wait to speak to someone. British Gas, AOL and DVLA kept people hanging on longest, with average waiting times of around three minutes. One call to AOL was held for over 15 minutes.

Then last year we found that the average wait to speak to someone on a broadband provider's technical support line is 1 minute 33 seconds. That actually sounds pretty good in my experience, but then the average wait to talk to someone at Plusnet did come in at nearly eight minutes.

Put tougher targets in place

Wouldn't those calls be so much more pleasant if calls were answered personally and directed through to the correct department immediately? It may sound too good to be true, but one foreign exchange broker, World First, has just announced a promise to do just that, answering with a human voice within three rings.

No, I've never heard of them either, so it's not going to make the blindest bit of difference to my waiting times, but it does make me wonder why more companies can't do the same – or at least put better policies in place to answering quicker.

Our own customer services team at Which? say it takes around a minute to get through our automated questions, but they aim to answer 80% of calls within 60 seconds after that. I wonder how many of the bigger organisations we have to deal with on a regular basis have similar targets?

I applaud World First, and almost wish I was a customer, but I won't hold my breath for others to follow their lead. For now, clearer options and a commitment to answering calls quicker would go some way to making this caller happier as she waits.

10 December 2010

⇨ The above information is reprinted with kind permission from Which? Visit www.which.co.uk for more information.

WHICH?

OFT warning on misleading pricing practices

The OFT today urged businesses to review their use of common pricing practices to ensure they comply with fair trading laws, or risk enforcement action.

The message follows the publication of an OFT market study into the advertising of prices, which established that certain pricing techniques used online, in-store and in adverts can mislead consumers, potentially breaching the law.

Advertising of prices is a key part of active price competition, which benefits both consumers and the economy. But evidence obtained by the OFT from consumer surveys, focus groups, psychology literature and groundbreaking behavioural economics research suggests that certain pricing techniques can lead consumers into purchasing decisions they would not have made were prices more clearly advertised, or to spend more than they need to.

The practices the OFT identified as having the greatest potential to cause harm are drip pricing (where optional or compulsory price increments are added during the buying process such as taxes, card charges and delivery charges), time-limited offers (such as 'offer ends today') and baiting sales (having only a small proportion of stock available at the advertised offer price). However, this does not mean that the use of these practices is automatically unlawful – this will depend on the specifics of the advert and a number of other factors.

Okay...
that's £14.50 for the repair,
plus £498.00 for the call out,
£53.50 for damp money,
less 75p for the tea and scones,
thank you.

This research has helped the OFT determine how it proposes to apply the Consumer Protection from Unfair Trading Regulations 2008, which prohibit, amongst other things, misleading advertising. Breaches of the regulations can result in court action and fines.

The OFT recognises that most businesses want to play fair with their customers and to comply with the law. In order to help them, it has published a new framework which sets out the criteria it will use in prioritising enforcement action against traders engaged in pricing practices causing the most harm to consumers.

On drip pricing, for example, businesses that ensure all compulsory charges are included in the headline price, and make details of all genuinely optional charges available at the early stages of the buying process are less likely to be subject to OFT enforcement action.

Fair dealing businesses should not be concerned that they risk enforcement action on trivial matters, and will benefit from clarity about the OFT's position. However, the OFT is actively monitoring price promotions and, where necessary, will take targeted national enforcement action against firms using practices that constitute serious breaches of the law.

In its national consumer protection role, the OFT's analysis is also designed to provide a lead for the compliance and enforcement work of local trading standards services and sector regulators.

John Fingleton, OFT Chief Executive, said:

'Pricing practices, used in a transparent and fair manner, can provide consumers with a helpful shortcut to assess whether a particular offer is a good or bad deal. However, our research has highlighted how certain pricing tactics can be used in a misleading way.

'Misleading pricing is not only bad for the consumer, it is also bad for competition, and creates an uneven playing field between fair-dealing businesses that stick to the spirit of the law, and those that push the boundaries too far.

'We urge all firms to review their pricing practices and to get their houses in order where necessary.'

2 December 2010

⇨ The above information is reprinted with kind permission from the Office of Fair Trading. Visit www.oft.gov.uk for more information.

© Office of Fair Trading

OFFICE OF FAIR TRADING

Are consumers turning away from credit?

Information from Money Facts.

The amount of credit given to consumers fell in 2010, with only car finance increasing last year.

Credit card spending fell by 7% in 2010, while the value of unsecured loans approved by lenders dropped by almost a quarter (24%), according to figures from the Finance & Leasing Association (FLA).

Spending on store cards also fell last year, with shoppers reducing their use of the products by 7% compared with 2009.

The only area of consumer credit that expanded last year was the car finance market.

The area was buoyant last year, growing by 9%, helping to inflate the overall figures. Without the positive figures in the car finance market, consumer credit would have fallen by 10% during 2010.

Credit card spending fell by 7% in 2010, while the value of unsecured loans approved by lenders dropped by almost a quarter (24%)

In December – traditionally a month when more customers use credit for some of their Christmas spending – there was a fall in credit sales. Credit card spending was down by 5%, whilst store cards and store instalment credit fell by more than a quarter each.

The figures reflect a difficult month on the High Street, with poorer than expected Christmas sales.

For the second consecutive month, the take-up of personal loans increased annually, although lending in this area was very low in December 2009.

'These figures confirm that there is no such thing as easy credit,' Fiona Hoyle, FLA head of consumer finance, said.

'Stricter lending requirements under the new EU Consumer Credit Directive mean that some consumers are finding it harder to access credit. Low consumer confidence is also a major factor in this fall in lending'

'Stricter lending requirements under the new EU Consumer Credit Directive mean that some consumers are finding it harder to access credit. Low consumer confidence is also a major factor in this fall in lending.

'Against this background of reduced lending and declining consumer confidence, the Government needs to be careful not to regulate some kinds of credit out of the market.

'For example, current proposals to restrict the store card sector could have serious repercussions for a High Street recovery and adversely affect customers with modest credit needs.'

24 February 2011

⇨ The above information is reprinted with kind permission from Moneyfacts. Visit www.moneyfacts. co.uk for more information.

© *Moneyfacts*

Consumers deserve more credit, says Which?

Information from Which?

Credit card companies are regularly giving consumers false or misleading information when they call to make a credit card claim enquiry, according to new research from Which?

In an undercover investigation*, the consumer champion found that 71 out of 120 calls to credit card companies failed to give researchers useful and correct advice about making a claim.

Mystery shoppers called the 12 biggest credit card providers to ask on behalf of a friend or relative about making a claim for goods bought or ordered using a credit card. Only ten out of the 120 advisers mentioned Section 75 or the Consumer Credit Act by name, and our researcher was given the correct money limits for claiming on Section 75 in just one of the 120 calls.

Many of our researchers were given incorrect information about where they could reclaim their money or get more help. Lloyds TSB told the caller to contact the Ministry of Justice, Barclaycard recommended their local authority and NatWest suggested pursuing the claim for an undelivered sofa through ATOL, the insurance scheme that covers airline failure.

Although there is no time limit to putting in a Section 75 claim, many advisers cited the Visa chargeback time limit of 120 days, and one Lloyds TSB adviser even quoted a week.

Tesco and Nationwide were particularly poor – not one call to them passed the Which? test. Our researchers found HSBC staff particularly unhelpful. MBNA were the least worst, passing our test in seven out of ten calls, more than any other firm.

Which? Chief Executive Peter Vicary-Smith says:

'It's not as if the rules on credit card claims are complicated. This situation is unacceptable – companies must accept that advice really matters. Consumers are potentially missing out on money they're owed because they've been misinformed. The industry must know the rules, and it shouldn't be up to the consumer to remind them of their rights.'

Which? is writing to each of the 12 credit card providers we investigated to suggest ways they can improve the information they give consumers.

> **'Consumers are potentially missing out on money they're owed because they've been misinformed. The industry must know the rules, and it shouldn't be up to the consumer to remind them of their rights'**

People who want to make a claim against their credit card provider, can find sample letters at www.which.co.uk/s75

For more information visit www.which.co.uk/money

Notes

* In November 2010 our mystery shoppers called the 12 biggest credit card providers asking for general advice on behalf of a friend or relative who hadn't had their order delivered after buying goods using a credit card. We made five calls to each provider about a problem buying a laptop online and five calls about buying a sofa on the high street.

The full article, 'Credit card claims', appears in the February 2011 issue of *Which?* magazine. For further information, a copy of the full article, or an interview, please contact Alice Lythgoe-Goldstein. To pass the Which? test, call centre staff had to give the fieldworker

useful and correct information about putting in a claim. A company could still pass if the representative said he or she did not know the answer, but would refer the call to a specialist team, provided the specialist team then met our criteria. If a representative gave incorrect or misleading information, this was treated as a fail. A neutral rating indicated that the mystery shopper was not given incorrect information, but the call centre staff were insufficiently helpful or knowledgeable to earn a pass

Ten facts about credit card protection

1 Under section 75 of the Consumer Credit Act, the card company is 'jointly and severally liable' for any breach of contract or misrepresentation by the company. You don't have to reach stalemate with (or take legal action against) the retailer before you claim against your card company.

Credit card companies are regularly giving consumers false or misleading information when they call to make a credit card claim enquiry, according to new research from Which?

2 S75 applies to items costing more than £100 and up to £30,000. It also covers reasonable costs you have as a result of the trader's breach of contract.

3 S75 is particularly useful if the retailer or trader has gone bust or doesn't respond to your letters or phone calls.

4 Items that you bought online or while overseas are also covered under s75.

5 S75 doesn't apply to purchases made using a credit card cheque or if you withdraw cash on your credit card to pay for an item or service.

6 S75 covers the whole purchase, even if you paid only part of the cost on the card and the rest by other means.

7 There is no time limit to putting in a s75 claim, but see also the facts above.

8 If the credit card company does not help, you can take your complaint to the Financial Ombudsman Service free of charge.

9 Chargeback is a useful industry-backed system for when s75 doesn't apply. This could be, for example, where you've paid by debit card or bought goods for less than £100.

10 There is a short time limit on chargeback claims. Visa, for example, sets a 120-day time limit which starts from the day that you are aware of a problem.

Which? is a consumer champion. We work to make things better for consumers. Our advice helps them make informed decisions. Our campaigns make people's lives fairer, simpler and safer. Our services and products put consumers' needs first to bring them better value.

23 January 2011

⇨ The above information is reprinted with kind permission from Which?. Visit www.which.co.uk for more information.

© Which?

Which industries, if any, would you say have responded particularly well to the economic downturn in the way they treat their customers?

Don't know – 28%
Supermarkets – 53%
High street chains – 21%
Small retail shops – 15%
Online retailers – 9%
Banks – 8%
Car sales – 7%
Energy companies – 5%
Mobile phone service providers – 4%
Travel agents – 4%
Airlines – 4%

Among the following types of business which three in your experience are the most likely to give you a fair deal?

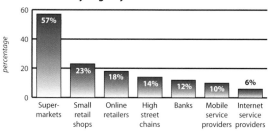

Super-markets	Small retail shops	Online retailers	High street chains	Banks	Mobile service providers	Internet service providers
57%	23%	18%	14%	12%	10%	6%

Research conducted by Ipsos MORI on behalf of Consumer Focus, between 23 and 29 January 2009, among a sample of 1,988 adults in GB

Which organisations and sectors do you see as leading the way in delivering excellent service to their customers?

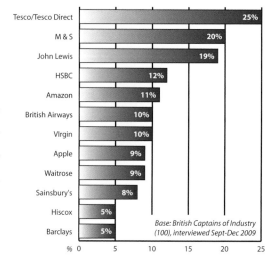

Tesco/Tesco Direct	25%
M & S	20%
John Lewis	19%
HSBC	12%
Amazon	11%
British Airways	10%
Virgin	10%
Apple	9%
Waitrose	9%
Sainsbury's	8%
Hiscox	5%
Barclays	5%

Base: British Captains of Industry (100), interviewed Sept-Dec 2009

Source: The Logic Group Loyalty Report 2010: The British Customer in 2010. The Logic Group/Ipsos MORI 2010

WHICH?

Identity fraud and identity theft

Identity theft is when your personal details are stolen and identity fraud is when those details are used to commit fraud.

More about identity fraud and identity theft

Identity fraud

Identity fraud can happen when:

⇨ fraudsters use a false identity or somebody else's identity details to obtain goods or services by deception;

⇨ criminals use genuine but falsely obtained documents, such as other people's passports or national insurance cards, to travel or to get public sector and welfare services;

⇨ identity information belonging to an individual or organisation is used to open accounts or apply for credit;

⇨ a fraudster uses identity details to produce counterfeit documents.

Fraudsters can use your identity details to:

⇨ open bank accounts;

⇨ obtain credit cards, loans and state benefits;

⇨ order goods in your name;

⇨ take over your existing accounts;

⇨ obtain genuine documents such as passports and driving licences in your name.

Stealing an individual's identity details does not, on its own, constitute identity fraud. But using that identity for any of the above activities does.

Identity theft

Identity theft is when someone's personal details, such as their name, date of birth, current or previous addresses are used without their knowledge or consent.

Also known as 'impersonation fraud', identity theft happens when fraudsters access enough information about someone's identity to commit identity fraud. Identity theft can take place whether the fraud victim is dead or alive.

If you're a victim of identity theft, it can lead to fraud that can have a direct impact on your personal finances and could also make it difficult for you to obtain loans, credit cards or a mortgage until the matter is resolved.

What's more, it costs the government and financial services industry many millions of pounds every year.

Your identity can be stolen in a number of ways:

⇨ A thief finds out your bank details or sees information about you on your bank or credit card statements or personal bills;

⇨ A thief finds out the personal details you've provided to online shopping sites and social networking sites, or finds them from other sources, such as births and deaths registers, etc.;

⇨ You might reveal enough personal information by replying to a fraudulent email, e.g. an email advising you have won a prize in a foreign lottery.

Are you a victim of identity fraud?

You may already be a victim of identity fraudsters if:

⇨ you have lost, or had stolen, important documents such as your passport or driving licence;

⇨ you've not received the post you expected from your bank;

⇨ items appear on your bank or credit card statements that you don't recognise;

⇨ you identify entries on your credit file from organisations you don't normally deal with;

⇨ you apply for a state benefit but are told you're already claiming it;

⇨ you receive bills, invoices or receipts addressed to you for things you haven't bought or services you haven't asked for;

⇨ you've been refused a credit card or a loan, even though you have a good credit history;

⇨ you discover a mobile phone contract has been set up in your name without your knowledge;

⇨ you receive letters from solicitors or debt collectors for debts that aren't yours;

⇨ financial institutions you don't normally deal with contact you about outstanding debts.

What should you do if you've been a victim of identity fraud?

⇨ Act quickly – you mustn't ignore the problem. Even though you didn't order those goods or open that bank account, the bad debts will end up under your name and address.

ACTION FRAUD

- If you believe you're a victim of identity fraud involving plastic cards (e.g. credit and debit cards), online banking or cheques, you must report it to your bank as soon as possible. Your bank will then be responsible for investigating the issue and they will report any case of criminal activity to the police. The police will then record your case and decide whether to carry out follow-up investigations.

- If you think you're a victim of another kind of identity fraud, you must report the matter to the relevant organisation. Depending on their advice, you should then alert your local police force. You should report all lost or stolen documents – such as passports, driving licences, plastic cards, cheque books – to the relevant organisation.

If you believe you're a victim of identity fraud involving plastic cards, online banking or cheques, you must report it to your bank as soon as possible

- If you're not sure which organisation to call, contact Action Fraud for advice.

- Contact Royal Mail if you suspect your mail is being stolen or that a mail redirection has been fraudulently set up on your address. The Royal Mail has an investigation unit that will be able to help you.

- Get a copy of your credit file. Your personal credit file will show exactly which financial organisations have accessed your details. Help to keep your personal information secure by asking for a copy of your credit file from any of these credit reference agencies:
  - Callcredit
  - Equifax
  - Experian

- Look at your credit file closely. If you find entries from organisations you don't normally deal with, contact them immediately. Remember to keep a record of all your actions, including the people you've spoken to and when, and keep copies of all letters you send and receive.

- If you suspect someone else has used your personal details fraudulently, the Credit Reference Agencies' Victims of Fraud Service will help you. Their service is free.

Protect yourself against identity fraud

- Don't throw out anything with your name, address or financial details without shredding it first.

- If you receive an unsolicited email or phone call from what appears to be your bank or building society asking for your security details, never reveal your full password, login details or account numbers. Most banks will not approach their customers in this manner.

- If you are concerned about the source of a call, ask the caller to give you a main switchboard number for you to be routed back to them. Alternatively, hang up and call your bank back on the legitimate phone number printed on your bank statements.

- Check your statements carefully and report anything suspicious to the financial institution concerned.

- If you're expecting a bank or credit card statement and it doesn't arrive, tell your bank or credit card company.

- Don't leave things like bills lying around for others to look at.

- Get regular copies of your credit report from a credit reference agency.

- If you move house, always get Royal Mail to redirect your post.

- The above information is reprinted with kind permission from Action Fraud. Visit www.actionfraud.org.uk for more information.

© Action Fraud

Fraud costs the UK over £38 billion, says the National Fraud Authority

Today [27 January, 2011] the National Fraud Authority (NFA) published its second Annual Fraud Indicator (AFI), which estimates fraud is costing the UK over £38 billion a year.

The new estimate and comprehensive data breakdown is testament to improved methodologies and cooperation across Government and industry. It also shows the real impact fraud has on individuals, businesses and Government.

Loss estimates to fraud by sector:

⇨ Public – £21 billion

⇨ Private – £12 billion

⇨ Individuals – £4 billion

⇨ Charity – £1.3 billion

The public sector remains the highest proportion of the fraud loss at £21 billion – 55% of the total figure. This estimate, for the first time, includes new and more accurate figures for procurement (£2.4 billion) and grant fraud (£515 million).

The size of the public sector estimate is, in part, due to diligence in reporting fraud loss data, combined with more comprehensive measurement techniques than other sectors. It is also important to note that this figure represents a relatively small percentage when taken in context of the public sector's overall spending and income.

A better understanding of fraud in the public sector has led to the Cabinet Office setting up a cross-Government Counter-Fraud Taskforce which is overseeing a number of pilots to develop and establish counter fraud techniques that can be rolled out across the public sector. In addition to this, the NFA is progressing 15 different projects, many of which form a part of the Taskforce work, to help central and local government cut key fraud risks and deliver savings.

Collaboration with the charity sector has enabled the NFA, for the first time, to provide an accurate estimate of the level of fraud within this sector. The £1.3 billion figure was identified in a survey the NFA conducted gauging how fraud affects the sector, to which over 1,000 charities responded. This estimate represents around 2.4% of the total charity sector turnover. The NFA and the Charity Commission are working closely together on a number of counter-fraud prevention initiatives to encourage charities to build improved fraud prevention measures into their operations and to develop a stronger counter fraud culture in this sector.

Private sector fraud losses of £12 billion make up 31% of the total annual figure.

⇨ The financial services industry recorded the highest loss to fraudsters at £3.6 billion. This is a slight decrease on the 2010 AFI figure of £3.8 billion due to improved fraud prevention methods involving plastic card (£440 million) and cheque fraud (£30 million).

⇨ Online banking, however, has seen an increase of 14% (£60 million). The sector continues to invest heavily in counter-fraud systems and solutions to help stay one step ahead of the criminals.

⇨ Mortgage fraud (£1 billion) and insurance fraud (£2.1 billion) remain high.

⇨ A new inclusion in the AFI is fraud losses to SMEs at £780 million. The NFA and the Federation of Small Businesses (FSB) worked together to produce this estimate – the first of its kind. It is hoped that raising awareness of the scale of loss will spur new fraud prevention initiatives in this sector.

Individual citizens' losses equated to 10% of the overall fraud figure (£4 billion), covering loss from mass-marketing fraud such as share sale, lottery and advanced fee frauds as well as newer frauds such as online ticketing and rental fraud. This additional information along with data included from Action Fraud, the national fraud reporting centre run by the NFA, widened the scope of last year's figure (£3.5 billion) to produce an increased figure within this AFI. Action Fraud saw over 70,000 contacts made by the public and 10,000 crimes reported totalling £93 million lost by individuals over the past 12 months to fraudsters.

The NFA and law enforcement are working together to build increased capacity for disruption of criminal attacks against individuals, as well as better intelligence sharing and analytics to support enforcement action. Cross-Government and industry work also continues to increase public awareness of fraud and how to protect against it.

Dr Bernard Herdan, Chief Executive of the NFA, said:

'Victims of fraud are found in all sections of society. Whether it is the public, private and charity sectors or as individual citizens, it is vital we join together to take action to stem the rising tide of fraud. The Annual

Fraud Indicator is our blueprint. It enables us to gain a perspective and judge the scale of the problem and target our actions accordingly.

'Tackling fraud will not solely be achieved through more investigation, prosecution and punishment of fraudsters. The NFA is working with its partners to promote greater fraud awareness and self-protection, encourage organisations to adopt fraud-proof systems, enable fraud reporting and facilitate better sharing of intelligence on fraudsters. We want to develop a stronger counter fraud culture, which helps to disrupt fraudulent activity across the UK and globally.'

Minister for the Cabinet Office Francis Maude said:

'The latest National Fraud Authority estimate shows that 55% of fraud – a massive £21 billion – is committed against the public sector. That's the equivalent of building 800 secondary schools, or employing over 615,000 nurses and it's a problem that we are not going to ignore. Ripping off the taxpayer will not be tolerated.

'Contrary to what many people think, fraud and error is not just confined to benefits and revenue. It affects every Government department and impacts on the Government's ability to deliver better public services, while stripping the civil service of vital resources. We can't and won't allow this to happen anymore. Our Counter Fraud Champions will begin work immediately to crack down on fraud across Government and public services.

'We know this zero tolerance approach works. The pilots being run by the Counter Fraud Taskforce, which I set up last year, are already making serious savings. HMRC has already saved £1 million from stopping single person allowance fraud, where 300 people have been identified as actually living with a partner. If rolled out nationally, this exercise could save £500 million-£1 billion over the next 18 months.'

Sam Younger, Chief Executive of the Charity Commission, said:

'We have previously said that fraud in charities has been under-reported, which is reflected in today's report. However, it also shows that instances of charity fraud remain low and the public can be assured that the vast majority of charitable money is going straight to good causes. Whilst no system can guarantee that any charity or business will be totally protected against loss, charity trustees must make sure that they have strong financial controls in place to protect their charities. One of the ways they can do this is by using the advice and guidance on our website. Charity trustees must be more fraud aware, and I hope that today's report is a wake-up call to any charity who thinks it will never happen to them.'

Mike Cherry, Policy Chairman, Federation of Small Businesses, said:

'The Federation of Small Businesses (FSB) was pleased to collaborate with the National Fraud Authority in capturing the cost of fraud to small businesses – around £2,800 per business, per year. These costs can hamper enterprise for small firms when in fact the Government are looking to them for economic growth and job creation.

'The FSB is calling on small businesses to report fraud to the Action Fraud – in the knowledge that this information will be used to build up a full picture of fraud with prosecutions as a result. Despite public sector cuts, small businesses still need to see an improvement in the capability of the police when dealing with these issues locally. Importantly too, we must see an end to the "passing the buck" scenario when a fraud involves more than one police force.'

Individual citizens' losses equated to 10% of the overall fraud figure (£4 billion)

Commissioner Adrian Leppard, of the City of London Police, National Lead Force for Fraud, said:

'With the advancement of technology we find the nature of fraud is constantly evolving. But the key facts remain the same; fraud is costing the UK economy tens of billions of pounds and fraudsters are destroying the lives of thousands of people, young and old.

'In 2011 we must make sure we use all the weapons at our disposal to break the criminal networks and help prevent fraud in all corners of our society. In the National Fraud Intelligence Bureau (NFIB) the counter fraud community now has the most advanced police analytical system in the world ready to lead our fight against financial crime.'

Nick Starling, Director of General Insurance and Health at the Association of British Insurers, said:

'Every household and business pays the price for fraud. The cost of insurance fraud alone adds an extra £44 a year to the insurance costs of the average household. To protect honest customers, the insurance industry is intensifying its efforts to deter potential fraudsters, and detect more fraud. With many frauds cutting across different sectors, the National Fraud Authority has a crucial role to play in spearheading a coordinated national strategy to reduce the impact of fraud on the economy and people's lives.'

27 January 2011

⇨ The above information is reprinted with kind permission from the Attorney General's Office. Visit www.attorneygeneral.gov.uk for more information.

Ethical consumerism, how we got here

*By Rob Harrison, editor and co-founder of **Ethical Consumer**. This is a condensed version of two articles originally printed in issue 50 and issue 100.*

From a boycott of sugar by anti-slavery protesters, to Chinese campaigns against American goods in 1905, calls for consumers to act on political issues can be found throughout history. Early trade unionists in the USA produced 'best-buy' lists of unionised companies, and landless peasants in Ireland first coined the word 'boycott' in a campaign against oppressive landowners as far back as 1880.

In the 1970s and 80s, consumers and investors in the West developed increasingly sophisticated disinvestment and boycott campaigns against companies operating in apartheid South Africa. Coupled with retailer boycotts in South Africa itself, these peaceful but powerful forms of direct action are now widely acknowledged to have been instrumental in hastening the regime's demise.

The late 1980s saw a real explosion of interest in the political power of consumers choosing to act ethically. Green consumer guides became international best sellers on the wave of environmental consciousness which swept the globe. The fact that global environmental crises like ozone depletion could be clearly linked to individual acts such as a choice of hairspray also meant that broader ideas of consumer responsibility could no longer be ignored.

It was during this time that the Ethical Consumer project began life. We believed that Ethical Consumerism addressed a structural flaw in capitalism which, in a global market driven by profit, rewarded the least ethical producers and punished the best. This, we believed, was a system failure which we wanted to address, and we believed that it was essential to change the culture of 'price-only buying'. If the majority of consumers were asking more questions than just 'how much is it?', then the tendency to reward the most efficient employer of child labour simply melted away.

Globalisation

Since World War II, more of what we buy has been produced or manufactured overseas. At ECRA we argue that this 'globalisation of production' is one of the primary causes of the huge growth of ethical consumer behaviour. Globalisation means that people concerned about social or environmental issues can no longer, in many cases, just lobby their own government. The UK Government simply has no power to ban child labour in Pakistan or prevent whaling by Icelandic fishing boats. Because of this, campaign groups concerned about such issues have been increasingly looking for active consumers to help put pressure directly on the companies involved. Pressure groups such as Christian Aid or Greenpeace have been the key players in the movement towards ethical consumerism.

The growth of consumer power

Another reason behind the growth of ethical consumerism is that these campaign approaches have actually been extraordinarily effective. When campaign groups opposed to animal testing began to organise consumer boycotts back in the late 1980s, three of the world's four biggest cosmetics companies were forced to abandon at least some types of testing within three years.

The most graphic example of consumer power in the 1990s occurred when Shell was forced into a dramatic climbdown over its decision to dispose of the Brent Spa oil platform in the North Sea. Although it denied that consumer pressure affected its decision, it cannot have

been coincidental that sales in some German outlets had dropped by 70% during the boycott campaign.

In the UK, consumers' resounding rejection of genetically modified foods in 1999 resulted in a number of large multinationals also rejecting the technology within their UK products, and expanding out into organic products instead.

£36 billion was the value of UK ethical consumerism in 2008. This compares to just £13.5 billion in 1999

Since we first started Ethical Consumer, there has been a real change in public understanding of the damaging behaviours of big business. This has partly emerged through high-profile antiglobalisation (now better known as global justice) protests and from high profile films and books such as *Supersize Me* and *The Corporation*.

Greenwash?

Since the late nineties, many companies have begun to market their products as ethical and begun to develop, sometimes sophisticated, corporate social responsibility (CSR) strategies. Often such claims have rightly been pilloried as greenwash and met with cynicism. Even so, there is still a significant difference between the best and worst multinationals in relation to ethical issues and there definitely is a core of companies whose intentions are genuine. The old certainty – that all big business is equally bad – is becoming less and less tenable, making ethical purchasing an even more effective tool for change.

A force for change

Despite, or perhaps because of, all the changes that have taken place since our inception in 1989, our core purpose here at Ethical Consumer looks like it will remain as relevant as ever. Since issue 1 we have argued that for individual citizens to be effective political actors, they need good quality intelligence about which corporations are really their friends and which are their enemies. Whether the next ten years brings forth a nuclear era, more biotechnology and nanotechnology, or simply continued gross injustice, we cannot lobby effectively for change if we are simultaneously funding our most pernicious opponents on our trips to the shops.

For as long as markets remain globalised, consumers will need to look beyond price to prevent the most malign corporations from taking the driving seat and from 'capturing' democratic governments along the

way. The three-quarters of consumers who tell pollsters that they care about ethical issues enough to purchase ethical products wield huge amounts of spending power. So even though you may think that as an individual you don't have much power over company behaviour, it's important to remember that our combined spending is enormous. By making positive choices when you shop, you can bring about lasting change.

You are not alone (ethical consumerism in numbers)

It's easy to get the idea that the odds are against us. However, if we look back over the years, we can see that tremendous changes have occurred, from the growth of ethical investment to the shift in company policies on GM foods. We believe that our work at Ethical Consumer has helped to bring out these changes and that there are many other successes worth celebrating.

⇨ **£36 billion** Value of UK ethical consumerism in 2008. This compares to just £13.5 billion in 1999.

⇨ Each UK household spends on average **£251 per annum** on green items (2008 figures).

⇨ Spending on ethical food and drink has increased more than threefold from £1.9 billion in 1999 to **over £6 billion** in 2008.

⇨ **£1.8 billion** The amount that UK consumers spent on ethical personal products in 2008.

⇨ **£768 million** Estimated total UK vegetarian foods market in 2008.

⇨ **£1.986 million** Retail sales of organic food & drink in the UK in 2008.

⇨ **£800 million** Sales of products carrying the Fairtrade mark in 2009.

⇨ **7.5 million people** The number of people benefiting from Fairtrade in Latin America, Africa and Asia.

⇨ **3,000** Number of Fairtrade retail and catering products available in the UK (doubled from 2007 figures).

⇨ **£172 million** Spent on ethical clothing in 2008 (up from 29 million in 2007).

⇨ **13 March 2007** Date UK Government published its Climate Change Bill.

⇨ The above information is an extract from *Ethical Consumer: a beginner's guide* and is reprinted with permission from the Ethical Consumer Research Association. Visit www.ethicalconsumer.org for more.

© Ethical Consumer Research Association

How to harness ethical shopping's 'floating voters'

Ever since they first entered public consciousness in the late 1980s, a great deal of time and money has been spent pondering the mysteries of the ethical shopper. How many of them are there? How influential are they? Where do they shop and what makes them tick?

Today, ethical trade is going mainstream. Most leading retailers now have global teams dedicated to it, while some have made ethical values central to their brand. But the ethical consumer – that is, the shopper for whom ethical considerations are a determining factor in their buying habits – remains an elusive figure.

The truth is, ethical consumers are still very much in the minority. Indeed, the latest research suggests that 'principled pioneers' and 'vocal activists' – those who campaign on ethical issues and fundamentally embed these values into their lifestyles – make up just eight per cent of the population.

For the rest of us, price and quality remain the key drivers of consumer choice on the high street.

So should we conclude from this that most ordinary shoppers simply don't care?

There's certainly a small group of 'deniers' who prefer to stick their head in the sand. According to our research, they have become a niche market in their own right.

But then there are the people in the middle. These are ordinary, decent people with busy lives, who believe the brands they trust play fairly, and will assume that this is so until someone – the media, or a campaign group, or even a friend or neighbour – tells them otherwise. For them, the ethics of their favourite retailers are a question not of demand, but of expectation.

These are the 'conveniently conscious' shoppers – the ones who want to do the right thing as long as you make it easy for them. Most of us probably belong in this bracket.

In fact, brands and retailers are far more interested in these 'floating voters' of ethical shopping than they are the ethical activists – or the ostriches, for that matter.

In today's fiercely competitive marketplace, brand capital – the feelgood values and associations consumers attach to the companies they're loyal to – can be critical. So while ethics may be just one among a whole package of expectations the consumer holds, if they feel a company has let them down in this area, the resulting breakdown in trust might just be enough to tip the balance in a rival's favour.

What does all this mean for an organisation like ETI? Unlike Fairtrade, ethical trade is not a consumer-facing proposition. We do not have a product range to offer, nor can we provide a simple action through which consumers can cast their vote for better international labour standards.

Our mission is to improve the working lives of poor and vulnerable people and it is businesses, rather than consumers, that we engage with in order to achieve this. Our work is by its nature incremental, and while we expect our members to make measurable progress, this doesn't always result in outcomes that resonate immediately with consumers or that help them negotiate the ethical shopping maze.

> *The latest research suggests that 'principled pioneers' and 'vocal activists' – those who campaign on ethical issues and fundamentally embed these values into their lifestyles – make up just eight per cent of the population*

Earlier this year ETI commissioned research to help us better understand these issues from the perspectives of both companies and consumers. The findings revealed a hunger for information about the sourcing practices of high street retailers. In particular, consumers are receptive to positive messages from the brands they are loyal to.

This is not to say that they welcome spin – today's sophisticated consumers can spot that a mile off. What they do want, they tell us, is clear, simple information and honest, realistic messages. They respect communications that do not overclaim, and which focus on tangible achievements. They don't expect companies' supply chains to be perfect, but they do want to know that they're doing what they can to make things better.

As ethical claims proliferate, there is a risk that consumer trust in them will diminish. For our part, ETI's tripartite constitution puts us in a unique position to bring balance and context to the ethical trade debate. We can support our members to find robust and credible

ways to communicate their commitment to ethical trade. Our NGO and trade union members can also help to illuminate what good practice looks like, and to guide public understanding so that consumers can make more informed judgements.

We will not defend companies unless they walk their talk. Equally, we will challenge critics of ethical trade who oversimplify the issues, or who think that there are easy fixes.

Positive, realistic communications between companies and their customers can only be good for ethical trade. The more companies are able to share their achievements, the more they will be motivated to keep raising the bar. This virtuous circle can only pay dividends for workers.

14 December 2010

⇨ The above information is reprinted with kind permission from the Ethical Trading Initiative. Visit www. ethicaltrade.org for more information.

© *Ethical Trading Initiative*

Life without supermarkets: escaping choice overload

Laura Laker discovers the joys of farmers' markets, the convenience of vegboxes, and the horror of plans for a nearby Tesco Metro that will threaten her local corner shop.

Flyers have started appearing all over my neighbourhood opposing plans for a Tesco Metro almost next door to my local corner shop.

I went in search of the shop owner, who I found looking tired and distracted. 'It's killing us,' he said, as we stood outside the shop, gazing into the middle distance like two people witnessing the end of an era. 'This big company will take half my customers. I employ ten people. In the end it will be just me.'

'I am sure Tesco really needs that money,' he added, bitterly.

A recent UN biodiversity report suggests large corporations' profits are ultimately paid for by societies and ecosystems, which suffer reduced quality of life and environmental and social degradation.

I couldn't help thinking that when a supermarket moves in, communities lose local biodiversity, too, and whatever price savings we may benefit from are paid for in lost jobs.

The council seems to have little power in this situation, regardless of how councillors may feel about it. Bizarrely, the petition cannot oppose the effect on local businesses, only how the new Tesco would affect local traffic flow with its obligatory parking spaces and lorry deliveries.

Choice overload

Wandering into a Tesco Extra last week I was shocked by the Tardis-like hell of aisles stretching to the horizon, and the 15 checkouts jammed with dazed shoppers. After months of small-scale shopping this grocery purgatory, with proud references to the store's support of 'local' initiatives, seemed decidedly surreal. I left empty-handed, but not before noticing with pity the harassed faces, seemingly overwhelmed with choice.

I could never fathom the supermarket vegetable sections, and gave up trying a long time ago. I would circle the aisles endlessly, rarely alighting on anything vaguely useful, and often coming away with only a bag of tangerines and some potatoes.

I now live above a dry-cleaner, whose staff receive my vegbox while I'm at work. This fantastic service of surprise vegetable delivery is a bit like having a nutritionist turn up at my door each week. I'd like to think I'm healthier for it.

Shop around

It seems ridiculous, but since using the local shops I suddenly started thinking things like: 'Rubber gloves! Where on Earth will I find rubber gloves?' I had no idea whether such things existed outside of supermarkets. I've since learned that shopping around is not only fruitful, but endlessly entertaining.

Two new farmers' markets have opened in my area alone in the last month, and I love the novelty of buying food outdoors, and tasting local, organic wine at 11am on a Saturday. Last weekend I met a woman who cycled her delicious spelt bread four miles from Walthamstow in a trailer; I learned about farmed mushrooms and bought one of the tastiest lettuces my friends and I have ever eaten.

It's fantastic to be so connected with your region, to know all these small industries are busily producing real, good quality food year-round, and to support them.

14 June 2010

© *The Ecologist*

Shoppers: put your money where your mouth is

Plenty welcome the arrival of a new supermarket, but those who don't should spend more at the local shops they value.

By Dave Hill

They're on my east London patch all the time: large vans, often unavoidably double-parked, emblazoned with the legends 'Sainsbury's', 'Ocado' or 'Tesco'. From these emerge men bearing heavy plastic crates who head for the neighbourhood's smarter front doors. Home food deliveries by supermarket giants are part of life's routine among the local, over-busy affluent. I wonder how many of these are opposed to the arrival of a Tesco Express just down the road, even as employees of the same company or others like it to unload produce into their halls. Maybe quite a few.

This scenario, with its whisper of a double standard, captures the challenge for the sorts of concerned citizen all across the land that regard the expansion of supermarkets into corner shop country as a menace to society. They foresee small independent traders driven out of business, the demoralising sight of boarded-up shop fronts and the homogenisation of neighbourhoods. They resent the economic and legal muscle with which the super-chains see off opposition and bemoan the inability of local authorities to stop them. They organise protests accordingly.

I sympathise. But the problem with people objecting to the success of supermarket chains is that in so doing they're also objecting to the consumer decisions other people make. We can argue that the dominance of a handful of food monsters ends up limiting choice, but not that anyone is forced to buy from a newly arrived supermarket in the first place. Unless Tesco has misjudged the market – not a failing for which it is renowned – it knows that plenty of folk from around my way will welcome it.

Tesco Express will surely score on price compared with independent competitors. This may not be so across the board but, as the butcher I use told me, if the giant round the corner makes an offer of two chickens for the price of one he'll struggle to match it. Bargains such as that make a big difference to people on tight incomes who are more likely to go out to do their shopping daily than to place a three-figure order online once a week. Some complain that our independent mini-markets charge too much. Are they to be criticised if they prefer the cheaper newcomer? And what about Adam, commenting on my local blog?

'Can someone tell me where on Lower Clapton Road you can get decent organic meat and GENUINELY fresh fruit and veg (that hasn't been lying around for days) for a decent price? The quality and freshness of such items in the current local businesses is questionable.'

He thinks having a Tesco Express will be 'fantastic'. I think its imminent arrival has already created a fascinating test case. My nearest corner shop is, as my neighbour the top London blogger Emily Webber wrote, friendly, unique and eagerly responsive to the needs of its wide variety of customers.

> **The problem with people objecting to the success of supermarket chains is that in so doing they're also objecting to the consumer decisions other people make**

It's been preparing shrewdly for Tesco's opening: new services include refilling Ecover bottles, looking after parcels if they're delivered when you're out and, yes, bringing your grocery order to your home. Their delicatessen counter has enlarged and improved. They do posh coffee and homemade soup. The other day I caught a friend swooning over the six different types of mushroom on display. It has identified its own strengths and is making the most of them.

My friend the mushroom-fancier hopes that, in the end, we'll all be winners: that Tesco will inspire all the local independents to think harder about providing a better or different service and end up flourishing rather than dying. I hope he's right. But if he's wrong, then some of those predictions of disaster will come true. Unless and until some localist statute gives councils greater powers to control the composition of their high streets there's really only one weapon at the disposal of those who see the big supermarkets as a colonising threat. That is to do what I'm trying to do: reduce their dependency on supermarkets and spend more at the local independent shops they value. To mangle a metaphor, they must put more of their money where they also put their food.

24 January 2011

Retail myths

Are small independent shops being driven out of business and replaced by 'clone town' Britain?

The British Retail Consortium champions retailers of all types and sizes, big and small, food and non-food, online and bricks and mortar.

The combination of successful multiples and successful small retailers is vital to consumer choice, to the richness of the retail mix in our high streets and to local economies.

The good news is the independent retailing sector is actually very resilient. The Local Data Company's *Openings & Closures Report 2009* shows the number of 'comparison' (non-food) retail businesses grew by just over three per cent in 2009 but within that, the number of independents grew 5.6 per cent while multiples barely rose at all. Convenience retailing saw a similar pattern with independents rising in numbers by 5.7 per cent and multiples by a lesser 3.5 per cent. In particular, numbers of butchers and bakers rose.

They are surviving and thriving by offering their customers something different from and/or better than their bigger rivals. Identifying niche opportunities and then delivering a competitive, customer-friendly offer is still the key to success, regardless of size.

The term 'clone town' usually refers to high streets and shopping centres which are dominated by relatively well-known retail brands and where independent shops are poorly represented or completely absent. Have these dastardly 'clones' declared war on independent-led diversity, or are smaller shops beset by other problems which help to explain their decline?

There are at least three groups of factors which, together, have undoubtedly contributed to the uncertain outlook for many small retailers.

⇨ The first of these concerns is the cost of running and retaining retail property. While the larger multiples are increasingly able to negotiate turnover-based rents, smaller retailers are still stuck with upward-only rent reviews. Rents have been rising in real terms every year over the past decade, while the 2010 revaluation of commercial property inflated many retailers' rates bills sharply. When small operators in high-cost locations finally throw in the towel and vacate their shops, only the big brands can afford to take on the leases and other overheads.

⇨ The second group of issues includes the planning and transport constraints which now apply to many traditional shopping centres. Ease and speed of access are powerful influences on consumers when they are choosing where to shop. Expensive parking and restricted access to town centres tend to enhance the attractions of edge-of-town and suburban retail parks and shopping malls. Customer footfall then declines and small shops find themselves up against the dangerous combination of falling trade and rising overheads.

⇨ The third group of issues relates to the growing burden of regulation – something which affects all retailers but falls particularly heavily on the small operator. Over the past decade, thousands of new regulations, inspired in both Brussels and Westminster, have come into force which retailers must understand and observe. Research by small retailers' organisations suggests that regulation is an important influence on the profitability and longevity of their businesses.

⇨ The above information is reprinted with kind permission from the British Retail Consortium. Visit www.brc.org.uk for more information.

© British Retail Consortium

Cheer up! Competition is good for business.

WE STOCK EVERYTHING

Ethical labels add millions to cost of food

Millions of pounds is being added to Britain's food bill because of the cost of running the baffling array of ethical food labels, an investigation by the Daily Telegraph has shown.

By Harry Wallop, Consumer Affairs Editor

There are up to 80 different ethical and food assurance schemes, all of which can be used on packaging to help shoppers make a decision about what to buy.

They include those run by the Vegetarian Society, Freedom Food, Rainforest Alliance and Red Tractor, as well as 13 separate organic schemes.

It is estimated that about a fifth of all the food Britons consume has some ethical label on it. Almost all of the schemes charge a fee for food companies or farmers to use their logos on products. The cost of these charges is passed on to the customer in higher prices.

The Soil Association, the leading organic certification body, for instance, charges about £650 a year to a food company, while the Marine Stewardship Council, which promotes sustainable fishing, charges up to £1,200 a year. Freedom Food, a scheme run by the RSPCA, the animal charity, charges up to about £500.

Many charge a royalty fee on each item sold as well as, or instead of, an annual fee. This involves the food producers having to pay a small cut of the sale price.

These include a fee of 0.03 per cent levied by the Soil Association, 0.5 per cent by the Marine Stewardship Council, and 0.3 per cent levied by Freedom Food.

Red Tractor, the largest scheme – £10 billion of products bearing its logo sell each year – also charges a small royalty fee. It is run by Assured Food Standards, a venture between farmers, the food industry and retailers to promote British food. It guarantees the food processor has complied with welfare and food safety laws.

An analysis by the *Daily Telegraph* of the accounts of the leading schemes filed at Companies House, suggested that the fees from all schemes add tens of millions of pounds to Britain's food bill each year, even though the majority of consumers do not understand most of the labels.

All of the bodies that charge a fee said it went back into the administration of the voluntary schemes, with the RSPCA saying that three-quarters of the money raised went into marketing Freedom Foods.

Consumer experts said that the fees should be made more explicit to shoppers.

Ed Mayo, Secretary General of Co-operatives UK, and former Government consumer tsar, said: 'Consumers are baffled and bamboozled. The ethical labels play a valuable role, but like all business clubs, they should be open and transparent with the public. The Fairtrade Mark is probably the gold standard in terms of public trust and rigour. Other of the ethical labels have more to do if they are not to discredit what has become a valued and co-operative part of our shopping experience.'

Last month Which?, the watchdog, discovered that the majority of the labels were recognised by just 20 per cent of consumers, with many of those failing to define what the labels meant.

Lucy Yates, food expert at Consumer Focus, the Government watchdog, said: 'The array of ethical food labels on the market can make it confusing for consumers who are trying to do the right thing. Food producers need to think carefully about which accreditation schemes consumers trust and understand so that it is easier for shoppers to choose between different products.'

11 October 2010

THE TELEGRAPH

Purely extravagant

Consumers balk at high cost of organic.

Cost remains a strong deterrent against the purchase of organic goods for UK consumers, a new report from YouGov SixthSense reveals. In the same report it is shown that a significant number (13%) of UK consumers will only buy organic foods if they are locally sourced.

58% of UK consumers who avoid purchasing organic foods do so because of perceived high prices. Second to the issue of cost for the organic abstainer is a scepticism surrounding the benefits of eating organic: one in four consumers who don't buy organic do not think it is any better than non-organic food.

Despite issues of cost, 13% of UK consumers say that they only buy organic produce. These consumers are predominantly: affluent, Londoners, women aged 25 and over, educated, homeowners and in one-person households.

Commenting on the problem of cost for organic manufacturers, James McCoy, Research Director for YouGov SixthSense said, 'Suppliers have been working hard to sustain interest in organic foods throughout this period of financial instability; many organic lines are coming down in price, and in some cases are equal to, or cheaper than standard branded products.'

A key demographic for the organic market, women aged 25-39, are markedly cold in their attitude towards organic – 71% in this bracket are not buying organic produce on account of cost. Overall, 42% of consumers say that they would buy more organic if they could afford it, while one in three consumers depend on special offers in order to take advantage of organic options.

McCoy added, 'There is a notable level of consumer disdain directed towards organic and those who engage in the organic lifestyle, as one in five consumers believe that organic products are used as status symbols. For many, organic foods occasion a feeling of insecurity with 14% of consumers saying they feel "guilty" for not buying enough organic products.'

7 October 2010

⇨ The above information is reprinted with kind permission from YouGov. Visit www.yougov.com for more information.

UK consumers fail to follow through on their support for Corporate Social Responsibility

Many UK consumers would prefer to shop at stores with reputable ethics records that exhibit corporate social responsibility, but a much smaller number buy exclusively from companies whose ethics they agree with. The findings come as part of a recent report by YouGov SixthSense into the ethical shopping practices of UK consumers.

Seven out of ten shoppers say they like shopping with companies who 'visibly give something back to society' and 81% of UK consumers say that they do not like buying products from companies they disapprove of. Despite this, however, only 30% say they manage to buy solely from companies that conform to their ethical standards.

Corporate Social Responsibility (CSR) is a concept that seeks to bring business and manufacturing practices into line with widely accepted ethical standards so that companies' business practices are compatible with the rights and wellbeing of all members of the public sphere.

Half of UK consumers say that they would like to buy from companies that have a strong CSR programme in place. Yet, in a blow to rights watchdogs and charities that seek to ensure CSR is widely implemented, 61% of consumers say they hear a lot about the concept but 'nothing of any substance'.

Commenting on the report findings James McCoy, Research Director for YouGov SixthSense, said: 'Openly submitting to CSR norms can only help a company's reputation, but that high esteem does not transpose easily into financial rewards or a loyal consumer base, especially in a recessionary period. Awareness and consumption of Fair Trade products is high but only because Fair Trade practices have become *modus operandi* without unduly raising the cost of the product.'

9 September 2010

⇨ Information from YouGov. Visit www.yougov.com for more.

YOUGOV

The big names behind your food brands

Who owns whom? The ethical brands with big owners.

You may be familiar with Copella juice or Green & Black's chocolate, but new Which? research shows few people know the multinational corporations that are behind many ethical food brands.

Who owns ethical brands?

Many ethical-sounding brands are owned by large companies, but our research shows that the parent's name is rarely displayed on products from these ethical brands.

We surveyed 2,110 Which? members about ten popular ethical brands, and they knew only about one in ten of the brand owners. When we told them the parent companies, there was a mixed reaction. Some didn't mind, but others felt 'conned' or 'tricked'. One member said: 'I feel consumers are being misled.'

People feel differently towards ethical brands than they feel about the parent companies. In our poll, 71% associated Seeds of Change chocolate with environmental responsibility – in comparison with only 15% for its parent company, Mars. See if you can match the other parent companies to the brands with our quiz, below left.

The lure of ethical brands

In our survey, two-thirds rated environmental and ethical issues as important when deciding which brands to buy. But of the ten brands we looked at, eight didn't display their parent company's name on products.

This lack of clarity is repeated on the websites of these brands, which focus on the origins of the brand. Examples include Copella, launched in 1969 as a Suffolk-based family business that is now owned by PepsiCo, but Copella's website didn't mention PepsiCo anywhere when we checked.

According to retail expert Dr Fiona Ellis-Chadwick: 'Taking on a brand that's already established, with a strong image and customer base, can be an easy option for a large company – all the hard work's been done.'

Small brands can benefit

While many people feel tricked, parent companies can give brands stability. Professor Craig Smith, Chair in Ethics and Social Responsibility at Insead Business School, says: 'Parent companies can give ethical brands the resources they need to expand their business and promote ethical products and environmental issues to a wider audience.'

But some members were worried that large companies might be more concerned with profits than ethics.

Of the brands we contacted, all said that since the parent company's involvement their products, ethics and values have remained unchanged, and that their parent company supported the ethical values of the original brand.

25 January 2011

⇨ The above information is reprinted with kind permission from Which? Visit their website at www.which.co.uk for more information on this and other related topics.

© Which?

Test your knowledge: who owns whom?
Which parent company (left) is linked to which brand (right)? Answers at the bottom.

Parent company	Brand
Kraft	Rachel's Organic
PepsiCo	Innocent
Groupe Lactalis	Abel & Cole
Wellness Foods	Green & Black's
Lloyds Banking Group	Buxton
Unilever	Tyrrell's
Coca Cola	Seeds of Change
Nestle	Dorset Cereals
Mars	Copella
Langholm Capital	Ben & Jerry's

Kraft owns Green and Black's. PepsiCo owns Copella. Groupe Lactalis owns Rachel's Organic. Wellness Foods owns Dorset Cereals. Lloyds Banking Group is the majority shareholder in Abel & Cole. Unilever owns Ben & Jerry's. Coca Cola is the majority shareholder in Innocent. Nestle owns Buxton. Mars owns Seeds of Change. Langholm Capital is the majority shareholder in Tyrrell's.

Fairtrade FAQ

Information from the Fairtrade Foundation.

What is Fairtrade?

Fairtrade is about better prices, decent working conditions, local sustainability, and fair terms of trade for farmers and workers in the developing world. By requiring companies to pay sustainable prices (which must never fall lower than the market price), Fairtrade addresses the injustices of conventional trade, which traditionally discriminates against the poorest, weakest producers. It enables them to improve their position and have more control over their lives.

What is the Fairtrade Foundation?

The Fairtrade Foundation is a development organisation committed to tackling poverty and injustice through trade, and the UK member of Fairtrade Labelling Organisations International (FLO). The Foundation works with businesses, civil society organisations and individuals to improve the position of producer organisations in the South and to help them achieve sustainable improvements for their members and their communities. Certification and product labelling (through the FAIRTRADE Mark) are the primary tools for our development goals. The backing of organisations of producers and consumers in a citizen's movement for change is fundamental and integral to our work.

What is the FAIRTRADE Mark?

The FAIRTRADE Mark is an independent consumer label which appears on UK products as a guarantee that they have been certified against internationally agreed Fairtrade standards. It shares internationally recognised Fairtrade standards with initiatives in 20 other countries, working together globally with producer networks as Fairtrade Labelling Organisations International (FLO). The Mark indicates that the product has been certified to give a better deal to the producers involved – it does not act as an endorsement of an entire company's business practices.

How many Fairtrade products in the UK are there?

The Fairtrade Foundation has licensed over 3,000 Fairtrade certified products for sale through retail and catering outlets in the UK.

How big is the UK Fairtrade market?

The UK market is doubling in value every two years, and in 2007 reached an estimated retail value of £493 million. The UK is one of the world's leading Fairtrade markets, with more products and more awareness of Fairtrade than anywhere else. Around 20% of roast and ground coffee, and 20% of bananas sold in the UK are now Fairtrade.

What product categories does Fairtrade certify?

Internationally-agreed Fairtrade generic criteria exist for the following commodity products and in each category there is a list of approved producers maintained by a FLO register.

Food products:

⇨ Bananas

⇨ Cocoa

⇨ Coffee

⇨ Dried fruit

⇨ Fresh fruit and fresh vegetables

⇨ Honey

⇨ Juices

⇨ Nuts/oil seeds/oil

⇨ Quinoa

⇨ Rice

⇨ Spices

⇨ Sugar

⇨ Tea

⇨ Wine

Non-food products:

⇨ Beauty products

⇨ Cotton

⇨ Cut flowers

⇨ Ornamental plants

⇨ Sports balls

How much of the price we pay for Fairtrade products goes back to the producers?

Whatever the price of the product on the shelf, only the FAIRTRADE Mark ensures that the producers have received what has been agreed to be a fairer price, as well as the social premiums to invest in the future of their communities. The Fairtrade price applies at the point where the producer organisation sells to the next person in the supply chain (usually an exporter or importer). It is not calculated as a proportion of the final retail price, which is negotiated between the product manufacturer and the retailer.

⇨ Information from the Fairtrade Foundation. Visit www. fairtrade.org.uk for more.

© Fairtrade Foundation

New research finds Fair Trade movement is a distraction, not a solution

In a new research paper released today, the Institute of Economic Affairs argues that claims by the Fair Trade movement are seriously exaggerated.

⇨ Fair Trade's selling point to customers is that by paying a premium and buying certified products they will help producers in developing countries. Although at the margins this may be true, research shows that fair trade is not a strategy for long-term development – conventional trade is often more effective. Yet campaigners expend a huge amount of time and resource into persuading people that Fair Trade is more successful than conventional trade in helping those in the poorest countries.

⇨ Fair Trade is not a long-term development strategy and the model is not appropriate for all producers. Fair Trade's proponents need to adopt some humility and accept that it is a niche market designed to benefit some producers; and is only capable of achieving a very limited objective.

⇨ It is likely that producers end up with only a small fraction of the extra margin consumers pay. Other than with wholly inadequate case studies, Fair Trade promoters have never demonstrated how much of the additional price actually reaches producers. Even analysts sympathetic to the movement have suggested that only 25% of the premium reaches producers. No study ever produced has shown that the benefit to producers anything like matches the price premium paid.

⇨ In the UK, the top Fair Trade consuming market, Fair Trade labelled produce made up less than 0.5% of food and non-alcoholic drinks sales in 2007, so the overall contribution to the poor is tiny.

⇨ Fair Trade doesn't benefit the poorest producers due to heavy administration requirements and fees involved in becoming a certified producer. (The certification charge starts at $1,570 in the first year – an unaffordable sum for most producers in the poorest countries.)

⇨ Fair Trade does not focus on the poorest countries. Fair Trade penetration is greater in middle income countries, rather than in poor ones. The top four nations by Fair Trade certified producers in 2007 were Mexico, Colombia, Peru and South Africa. These nations had an average GDP per capita of $4,790 in 2007. The 13 nations with only one Fair Trade certified producer had average GDP per capita of just $2,807 in 2007. Coffee-producing countries with

no Fair Trade producers have an even lower average GDP per head. Most significantly, using data from 2005-07 for Fair Trade exports to the USA, it is not possible to find any significant negative relationship between national income per head or poverty and Fair Trade penetration.

⇨ Fair Trade's demand of exclusivity from schools etc. can damage other social labelling initiatives such as the Rainforest Alliance. Other such labelling initiatives often provide environmental and social benefits in a more direct way.

⇨ Fair Trade's consumers are given the impression that Fair Trade guarantees the price paid to producers. It does not, however, guarantee the quantity of produce that will be bought. Fair Trade has never been tested in adverse market conditions – the very conditions in which it is designed to help producers.

⇨ Fair Trade's requirements and the administrative burdens it imposes on poor producers often better reflect the prejudices of western consumers than the real needs of poor producers.

> ## *Fair Trade's selling point to customers is that by paying a premium and buying certified products they will help producers in developing countries*

Philip Booth, Editorial and Programme Director at the IEA, said:

'Proponents of Fair Trade are guilty of overstating the impact of their movement. Fair Trade products can squeeze out from the market other socially labelled products and place heavy burdens on companies when it comes to certification. In the long term helping those struggling in the poorest countries requires much more radical reform from within. Fair Trade is a niche part of the trade system and it should not be the focus of so much attention. Lifting communities out of poverty means allowing free trade to drive development and growth.'

4 November 2010

⇨ Information from the Institute of Economic Affairs. Visit www.iea.org.uk for more.

© *Institute of Economic Affairs*

INSTITUTE OF ECONOMIC AFFAIRS

Retail ethics and green retailing 2011: more than plastic bags?

The future of UK retailing – for the moment at least – is very green.

Retailers are keen to show that they are green, recycling-friendly, fair-trading, socially-responsible and energy-conserving.

It is easy to be cynical, but there are a lot of staff at ASDA, Coop, Tesco, M&S, B&Q who believe, and who want, their retail businesses to become greener. They also want to help their customers to become greener. This is not just tokenism. They really do believe it.

It is also good business.

There are several things that retailers can do:

1 They can change their operations to become greener retailers.

2 They can sell more socially-responsible and greener products.

3 They can promote improved lifestyles to their customers.

4 They can support fair trade socially-responsible organisations.

5 They can agitate for change.

YES BUT

The problem is that our consumer lifestyle is about Excess. How can retailing ever be green, when it normally involves people buying new things? How can leisure be green, or eating out, or green holidays?

Only a small proportion of people want radical change (although they may be happy to suggest it for others). So there is no point in retailers suggesting that everyone should become vegetarians or start mending their own clothes rather than buying something new. Based on what consumers seem to want, we are probably talking about a bit of hardship, some changes in the lifestyle, some environmental changes rather than a radical rethink of lifestyles.

Our conclusions

⇨ Greener shops. Most retailers are keen to show they are environmentally-conscious.

⇨ Green policies. Strategically, most large retailers are now committed to environmentalism through 'green policies', curbing waste, less packaging, product revamps, reduced energy use, fewer distribution trips, reducing product-miles by sourcing more products from the UK, and using greener energy for their own vehicles.

⇨ Retailers probably do far more to green their operations than the customer-facing bits of the store. Practically-invisible changes to transport, distribution, energy use, waste disposal and supply-factors are being made by most retailers and these are probably more sustainable than the bits the customers can see.

⇨ Retailers would do more if the green suppliers were there. Retailers are finding that the waste gathering/processing, biomass and energy saving industry is not yet sufficiently advanced to meet their requirements, so they are having to intervene in these industries themselves.

⇨ Humane food and fairtrade. There has been a shift in obtaining at least some foods from sustainable sources/humane treatment of animals/fairtrade. This can be patchy. The consumer is often more concerned about price than humane treatment.

⇨ Consumer information.

⇨ Packaging. Movement on packaging has been slower. Packaging protects goods. De-packaging is problematic if it increases waste and promotes crime. Retailers will make further progress.

⇨ Subsidies are a danger. Many retail green policies are helped by subsidies from the Government and some policies are only economic with those subsidies. We can expect some of these to be withdrawn in about five years and retailers must be aware of the likelihood of this occurring.

⇨ Greenwash is a danger. Customers and green organisations will be anxious to see that retailers carry out all their promises and will rub their noses in it if any are unfulfilled.

⇨ Environmental transparency. Customers will expect environmental transparency – 'prove your eggs are actually free range', 'prove your sweaters are not produced by slave labour' and expect the Internet to be used a great deal by savvy suppliers to prove this.

⇨ A green retail sector? Although farmers' markets have been successful and organic food stores less so, there is no evidence that new environmentally-friendly retailers stand much of a chance in creating new retail chains.

⇨ Information from the Centre for Retail Research. Visit www.retailresearch.org for more.

© Centre for Retail Research

Children and advertising

Information from the Advertising Standards Authority.

Protecting children has always been at the heart of our work: in 1962 – the ASA's very first year of operation – one of our priorities was to look into ads for horror films and their potential to scare children. Ensuring that children are not exposed to potentially harmful or inappropriate advertising has remained an ongoing commitment, a fact underlined by a recent public consultation on the Advertising Codes which resulted in enhanced protections for children being introduced.

Inexperience

Why does the advertising regulatory system place a particular emphasis on protecting young people? By virtue of their age and inexperience children are more credulous and vulnerable than grown-ups. They don't necessarily have the understanding of the commercial world or the consumer savvy possessed by most adults.

Therefore, the potential for an ad to mislead or harm a child is greater. As such, the advertising rules surrounding children are very strict. They state that ads shouldn't contain anything likely to result in their physical, mental or moral harm. There are also rules about the advertising of specific products such as gambling and alcohol, which set out to ensure that they are not advertised inappropriately at children.

Responding to societal concerns

Societal concerns about the effects of the commercial world on children are high on the political agenda. Government has established a Childhood and Families Task Force, chaired by the Prime Minister, and one of its aims is to address 'irresponsible advertising that sexualises children'.

The ASA shares the Government's priority to protect children, and while the Government's concerns seem to relate primarily to other forms of marketing that are not subject to the Advertising Codes, the ASA takes this issue very seriously and will not hesitate to tackle any advertiser that crosses the line.

Fortunately this is not a 'creative' route that advertisers commonly choose to take. The sexualisation of children is, of course, strictly prohibited by the Advertising Codes. For instance, no ad featuring a child or anyone who appears to be under 18 years of age should place them in a sexual context such as provocative or inappropriate poses and attire, overly 'made-up' or in states of undress. Historically, there are only a small handful of ads that have breached the rules on these grounds.

Appropriate targeting

But it is not just ads addressed to, targeted at or featuring children that have to adhere to the rules. Even when ads are aimed at an adult audience, advertisers have to take great care to target them appropriately and not cause harm or distress to children.

The ASA will take into account the context, the medium in which an ad appears and the audience when considering whether an ad is in breach of the Codes. The placement of an ad will have a direct bearing on whether the ASA will judge it to be acceptable. So an ad that might be acceptable if it appears in a magazine that was unlikely to be read by children might be considered unacceptable on a billboard.

A new media world

The ASA applies the rules robustly. But as different media converge and new marketing techniques emerge the regulatory system has to be responsive to, and keep pace with, new advertising trends in order to remain effective in protecting consumers and, in particular, children. The ASA already regulates SMS text ads, banner, tower and pop-up ads online, as well as paid search and viral advertising, but there are some types of online marketing that consumers complain to the ASA about, but we can't act upon.

In March 2010, the advertising industry formally recommended that the ASA's remit should be extended online to cover marketing communications on companies' own websites. This is a highly significant milestone for advertising regulation; addressing consumer and Government concerns about the regulatory gap online.

The potential for an ad to mislead or harm a child is greater. As such, the advertising rules surrounding children are very strict

The body responsible for writing the Advertising Code (the Committee of Advertising Practice) is currently working through the practicalities of these recommendations and we hope an announcement will be made in autumn this year. The digital remit extension will enable the ASA to apply the Code to those online marketing communications that currently sit outside our remit, providing protections that are well established across all other media and in online ads, for the benefit of consumers, children and industry.

Social responsibility

New Advertising Codes come into effect on 1 September and contain several new rules that are designed to afford further protections for children. For instance, a new scheduling restriction to prevent ads for age-restricted computer and console games from appearing around programmes made for, or likely to appeal particularly to children is being introduced. This will help to address concerns about depictions of violence or horror that are unsuitable for younger viewers.

New rules have been introduced about preventing marketers from collecting personal data from under-12s, without parental consent and preventing the collection of data about other people from under-16s. These rules set out to address concerns about privacy.

Perhaps most significantly, however, is the introduction of an over-arching social responsibility clause in the new Broadcast Code. On occasions where an ad adheres to the letter of the Code but runs contrary to the spirit in which it was intended and is, as a result, socially irresponsible, the ASA will be able to have it withdrawn.

This rule, which has existed for many years in the non-broadcast Advertising Code, provides a catch-all for the unexpected or unintended and will benefit all consumers. But it is especially important in providing a greater scope to the ASA to protect children.

It is unrealistic to prevent children from seeing ads at all. But the rules, and tough ASA action, ensure that the vast majority of ads that children see or hear are not inappropriate.

If you do see an ad that causes you concern under the Advertising Codes, please register a complaint.

⇨ The above information is reprinted with kind permission from the Advertising Standards Authority. Visit www.asa.org.uk for more information.

© *Advertising Standards Authority*

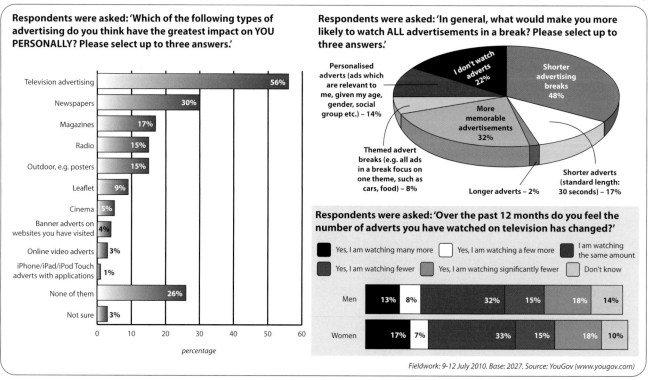

Respondents were asked: 'Which of the following types of advertising do you think have the greatest impact on YOU PERSONALLY? Please select up to three answers.'

	percentage
Television advertising	56%
Newspapers	30%
Magazines	17%
Radio	15%
Outdoor, e.g. posters	15%
Leaflet	9%
Cinema	5%
Banner adverts on websites you have visited	4%
Online video adverts	3%
iPhone/iPad/iPod Touch adverts with applications	1%
None of them	26%
Not sure	3%

Respondents were asked: 'In general, what would make you more likely to watch ALL advertisements in a break? Please select up to three answers.'

- Shorter advertising breaks 48%
- I don't watch adverts 22%
- More memorable advertisements 32%
- Shorter adverts (standard length: 30 seconds) – 17%
- Personalised adverts (ads which are relevant to me, given my age, gender, social group etc.) – 14%
- Longer adverts – 2%
- Themed advert breaks (e.g. all ads in a break focus on one theme, such as cars, food) – 8%

Respondents were asked: 'Over the past 12 months do you feel the number of adverts you have watched on television has changed?'

- ■ Yes, I am watching many more
- □ Yes, I am watching a few more
- ■ I am watching the same amount
- ■ Yes, I am watching fewer
- ■ Yes, I am watching significantly fewer
- □ Don't know

	Many more	A few more	Same amount	Fewer	Significantly fewer	Don't know
Men	13%	8%	32%	15%	18%	14%
Women	17%	7%	33%	15%	18%	10%

Fieldwork: 9-12 July 2010. Base: 2027. Source: YouGov (www.yougov.com)

The impact of the commercial world on children's wellbeing

Report of an independent assessment for the Department for Children, Schools and Families and the Department for Culture, Media and Sport – executive summary.

⇨ Children today are exposed to a growing number and range of commercial messages. These extend far beyond traditional media advertising, and involve activities such as online marketing, sponsorship and peer-to-peer marketing. Commercial forces also increasingly impact on children's experiences in areas such as broadcasting, education and play.

⇨ The commercial world offers children important opportunities in terms of entertainment, learning, creativity and cultural experience. But there are also significant concerns about what many see as harmful impacts on children's wellbeing, especially on their mental and physical health.

⇨ The debate on these issues is polarised and often sensationalised, making it hard to arrive at a balanced view. Commercialism needs to be understood in relation to broader changes in the economy and in family life, without succumbing to nostalgia for a mythical 'golden age'. Simple cause-and-effect explanations do not do justice to the complexity of the issues.

⇨ The evidence, both of risk and harm caused by the commercial world and of its benefits, is rarely conclusive. Overall, it suggests that children are neither the helpless victims imagined by some campaigners nor the autonomous 'savvy' consumers celebrated by some marketing people.

⇨ There is some research that establishes associations between aspects of the commercial world and negative wellbeing among children. However, in most key areas relating to physical and mental health there is very limited evidence of any causal relationship. Few studies have clearly established the importance of commercial factors as compared with other influences, such as parents and peers.

⇨ Equally, the commercial world may have a whole range of positive effects on children; but reliable evidence on specific impacts is very limited, and there is little or no independent evaluation of the claims of businesses in this respect.

⇨ New media and marketing techniques raise some ethical concerns about potential deception and threats to privacy: the public is not currently well-informed about this area, and existing regulation is insufficient in some respects.

⇨ Growing commercial pressures are undermining the production of UK-originated children's television programmes.

⇨ Schools and public spaces are increasingly being used as marketing venues and being affected by privatisation and commercialisation. The implications of these developments for children's wellbeing remain to be identified.

⇨ In these and other areas, commercialisation may accentuate inequalities and place further pressure on those who are already disadvantaged.

⇨ The commercial world is not going to disappear. Children and parents need to understand it and deal with it. Consumer and media literacy, both at home and in schools, offers one important strategy here, although it needs further evaluation.

December 2009

⇨ The above information is reprinted with kind permission from the Department for Children, Schools and Families. Visit www.dcms.gov.uk for more information.

© Crown copyright

DEPARTMENT FOR CHILDREN, SCHOOLS AND FAMILIES

The commercialisation of childhood

During the past decade, UK children have been exposed to an explosion of commercial activity, both within the home and in public places.

Developments in technologies such as mobile phones, computer gaming, multi-channel television and the Internet have given marketing and advertising industries direct access to youngsters like never before. Coupled with increased sponsorship deals in schools and the proliferation of branded play sites, those opportunities have extended still further.

But what impact is this having on the wellbeing of children and young people? Are they thriving in a creative and exciting environment – or is all this hard sell harming childhood? Alison Laing met Loughborough's Professor of Social Policy Research, Alan France, to discuss the hotly debated topic.

Growing concern in society about the impact of the commercial world on the wellbeing of children and young people has not gone unnoticed by Government. The subject recently prompted the Department for Children, Schools and Families (DCSF) to publish an independent report on the issue. Its remit was to gather and evaluate evidence about children's commercial engagement, the impact of this on their wellbeing, and the views of parents and children.

As part of the national report *The Impact of the Commercial World on Children's Wellbeing*, Loughborough University's Centre for Research in Social Policy (CRSP) and the Department of Social Sciences were commissioned to undertake a £30,000 study, specifically on the marketing and advertising industries' strategies towards children and young people. The six-month collaboration between researchers Professor Alan France, Graham Murdock and Jo Meredith involved an extensive literature review and analysis of the industry.

Professor France said: 'This is a really contentious area. There are two very different positions about the relationship children should have with the commercial world.

'Some say children should, and need, to engage with it, and that it's an important part of their learning process. They argue that children are incredibly savvy, and capable of understanding, assessing and making good judgements. And that it's the world they are going to enter as adults and therefore it's important not to legislate extensively in this area.

'On the other side, there is concern that concentrated exposure to commercial messages is eroding childhood as an open and diverse space for learning and development.'

Professor France added: 'Neither of those positions are very well evidenced, which is why the Government commissioned the assessment of knowledge in this area, so they can take decisions, make recommendations and develop policy.'

> **Developments in technologies such as mobile phones, computer gaming, multi-channel television and the Internet have given marketing and advertising industries direct access to youngsters like never before**

In their report, Professor France and his colleagues explain that the volume of commercial messages children and young people are exposed to has greatly increased during the past ten years.

LOUGHBOROUGH UNIVERSITY

One of the factors is down to the expansion of new digital media. The take-up of multi-channel television, the use of the Internet in homes, the growth of online and computer gaming and mobile phone usage among children of all ages has created new ways for marketing and advertising to access children.

Professor France said: 'There are a large proportion of five-year-olds today who have access to a mobile phone. We also know about 90 per cent of over 12-year-olds have access to one. From a marketer's point of view, that is a very useful way of talking to children in an unregulated format because mobile phones don't come under any legislation arrangement.

'Children also have much more choice about how they use the media available to them within their home. Children's bedrooms are more privatised spaces, and they are spending time alone there, making their own decisions about what they wish to watch, play and access. This makes them vulnerable to marketing and means they may view programmes and channels that are not necessarily suitable for their age group.'

Loughborough researchers identified gaps in the current regulation framework. While legislation exists around children's broadcasting and advertising (particularly with regard to foods high in sugar, salt and fat, and with recognised measures such as the 9pm watershed), far less regulation is applied to the Internet.

Tough rules in broadcasting alone are not enough, researchers noted. Regulation would need to be expanded and adapted to the changing realities of a converged, digital environment, in which marketers increasingly work across multiple platforms.

Professor France said: 'Another area that is unregulated is sponsorship. Schools and public spaces are increasingly being affected by privatisation and commercialisation. It's commonplace to see big providers such as Tesco, Sainsbury and Morrisons advertising in schools, and getting parents to purchase goods in exchange for vouchers for computer or gardening equipment.

'And then there is the growth of sponsored materials in schools. So we now start to see the likes of Nestlé or Procter and Gamble deliver science kits for the curriculum, Renault provide books, and Disney's High School Musical incorporate a dance CD into children's PE lessons.

'The companies would say it's for social good – but they are not doing all this for free.'

Professor France added: 'There has been a change in the types of play children engage in too, which creates new opportunities for marketers and advertisers. Play used to be going out into the street, now it is about going to commercial products such as computer game consoles.'

He concluded: 'There are some historical trends that have been with us for years – for example, product placement was around in the 1920s. But what we have been able to do is identify the new ways that marketing is operating with the new media that are emerging. It's brought everything up to date, which I think is really important and one of the real values of this report.

'Our review has highlighted a whole number of different techniques that have been introduced, but the evidence of its impact around children's wellbeing – for the better or worse – is weak.

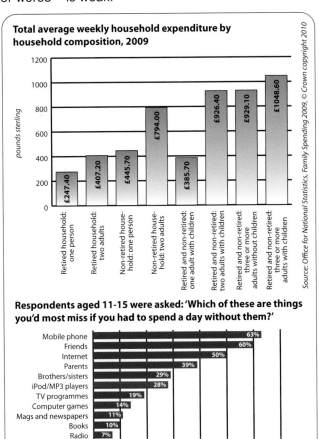

Total average weekly household expenditure by household composition, 2009

Source: Office for National Statistics, Family Spending 2009, © Crown copyright 2010

Respondents aged 11-15 were asked: 'Which of these are things you'd most miss if you had to spend a day without them?'

- Mobile phone 63%
- Friends 60%
- Internet 50%
- Parents 39%
- Brothers/sisters 29%
- iPod/MP3 players 28%
- TV programmes 19%
- Computer games 14%
- Mags and newspapers 11%
- Books 10%
- Radio 7%
- Teachers 1%
- Advertising 0%

Source: Children's Wellbeing In a Commercial World: A contribution by The Advertising Association to the DCSF enquiry. Advertising Association, January 2009

'The question for policy is how best to encourage children to take advantage of all this expanded choice, while protecting them from harm. It's now for Government to assess the findings and make decisions on what to do next.'

Spring/Summer 2010

⇨ The above information is taken from the spring/ summer 2010 edition of *The View*, published by Loughborough University, and is reprinted with permission. Visit www.loughborough.ac.uk for more information.

© *Loughborough University*

LOUGHBOROUGH UNIVERSITY

KEY FACTS

⇨ The retail industry employed over 2.9 million people as at the end of December 2009. This equates to 11% of the total UK workforce. (page 1)

⇨ Half the population now think consumers have more power to influence business. Three-quarters say they now make more of an effort to get the best deal. UK consumers are now leaving well over 100 million comments online every year. (page 3)

⇨ In a survey by Consumer Focus, 85 per cent of consumers said that the Internet makes it easier than ever to get the best deal. This isn't just the view of younger people: nine out of ten people (90 per cent) aged 55 and over agreed, more than any other age group. (page 4)

⇨ Shopaholics have an average personal shopping debt of £3,353 – nearly three times the national average. (page 6)

⇨ Of the £52.20 average weekly spend on food and non-alcoholic drink, almost three-quarters (72 per cent, £37.70 per week) was purchased from large supermarket chains. (page 7)

⇨ Average UK household had £174 a week of discretionary income in January 2011, 4.7 per cent lower than a year earlier. (page 8)

⇨ Town centre vacancy rates climbed from 12% at the end of 2009 to 14.5% at the end of 2010, according to the end of year report by the Local Data Company (LDC), which says that shops and shoppers are being hit by structural changes that threaten the future of the high street. (page 9)

⇨ Consumers from around the world feel strongly that store brands are the same as, or better than, national brands at providing a variety of benefits. (page 11)

⇨ Under Section 75 of the Consumer Credit Act 1974, if you pay for goods worth more than £100, even partially, on a credit card then the credit card company is equally liable with the retailer. (page 12)

⇨ British consumers are the most enthusiastic online shoppers in Europe, but one in four worries more about shopping this way than through traditional offline outlets, according to latest research. (page 13)

⇨ The average wait to speak to someone on a broadband provider's technical support line is 1 minute 33 seconds. (page 14)

⇨ In an undercover investigation, Which? found that 71 out of 120 calls to credit card companies failed to give researchers useful and correct advice about making a claim. (page 17)

⇨ Estimates suggest that fraud is costing the UK over £38 billion a year. (page 21)

⇨ Spending on ethical food and drink has increased more than threefold from £1.9 billion in 1999 to over £6 billion in 2008. (page 24)

⇨ It is estimated that about a fifth of all the food Britons consume has some ethical label on it. Almost all of the schemes charge a fee for food companies or farmers to use their logos on products. The cost of these charges is passed on to the customer in higher prices. (page 29)

⇨ 58% of UK consumers who avoid purchasing organic foods do so because of perceived high prices. (page 30)

⇨ People feel differently towards ethical brands than they feel about the parent companies. In our poll, 71% associated Seeds of Change chocolate with environmental responsibility – in comparison with only 15% for its parent company, Mars. (page 31)

⇨ The Fairtrade Foundation has licensed over 3,000 Fairtrade certified products for sale through retail and catering outlets in the UK. (page 32)

⇨ In the UK, the top Fair Trade consuming market, Fair Trade labelled produce made up less than 0.5% of food and non-alcoholic drinks sales in 2007. (page 33)

Advertising

Advertising is communication between sellers and potential buyers. This can be delivered by various media, including radio, television, magazines, newspapers, billboards and website banners.

Consumer

A consumer is anyone who purchases and uses goods and services.

Consumer rights

A consumer has the right to expect certain standards in the goods they buy. The law says that the goods must be of satisfactory quality, fit for their purpose and as described. These statutory rights cover all goods bought or hired from a trader, including goods bought in sales.

Credit

A consumer can obtain goods and services before payment, based on an agreement that payment will be made at some point in the future. Other conditions may also be imposed. Forms of credit can include personal loans, overdrafts, credit cards, store cards, interest-free credit and hire purchase. However, reliance on credit can result in high levels of consumer debt.

Economy

The way in which a region manages its resources. References to the 'national economy' indicate the financial situation of a country: how wealthy or prosperous it is.

Ethical consumerism

Buying things that are produced ethically – typically, things which do not involve harm to or exploitation of humans, animals or the environment; and also by refusing to buy products or services not made under these principles.

Expenditure

The act of paying out money.

Fair trade

Fair trade is about improving the income that goes to farm workers at the beginning of a supply chain, ensuring that they are paid a fair and stable price for the product supplied. Items produced using fair trade can be identified by the Fairtrade mark.

Fraud

The act of deceiving or conning someone for financial gain.

Gross Domestic Product (GDP)

The total value of the goods and services produced in a country within a year. This figure is used as a measure of a country's economic performance.

Interest

A fee charged on borrowed money. It is usually calculated as a percentage of the sum borrowed and paid in regular instalments. An 'interest rate' refers to the amount of money charged on a borrowed amount over a given period. Interest can also be earned on money which is deposited in a bank account and is paid regularly by the bank to the account holder.

Recession

A period during which economic activity has slowed, causing a reduction in Gross Domestic Product (GDP), employment, household incomes and business profits. If GDP shows a reduction over at least six months, a country is then said to be in recession. Recessions are caused by people spending less, businesses making less and banks being more reluctant to loan people money.

Scam

A scam is a scheme designed to trick consumers out of their money. Scams can take many forms, and are increasingly perpetrated over the Internet: 'phishing' scams, where a web user is sent an email claiming to be from their bank in order to gain access to their account, is one common example.

ACKNOWLEDGEMENTS

The publisher is grateful for permission to reproduce the following material.

While every care has been taken to trace and acknowledge copyright, the publisher tenders its apology for any accidental infringement or where copyright has proved untraceable. The publisher would be pleased to come to a suitable arrangement in any such case with the rightful owner.

Chapter One: Consumer Trends

The consumer in 2010, © The Consumer Council for Northern Ireland, *Retail key facts,* © British Retail Consortium, *The problem isn't consumption – it's Consumerism,* © Conservation Economy, *Unleashing the new consumer power,* © Consumer Focus, *Spend-emic hits British men and women,* © uSwitch, *Household spending falls for first time in ten years,* © Crown copyright is reproduced with the permission of Her Majesty's Stationery Office, *January's fall in family spending power beats records for second month in a row,* © Asda, *Empty shops are killing UK's high streets,* © Guardian News and Media Ltd 2011, *UK consumers continue to harbour unsafe online shopping habits,* © shopsafe.co.uk, *Disgruntled shoppers ditch online grocery services,* © shopsafe.co.uk, *Consumers see little difference between national and store brands,* © Ipsos MORI.

Chapter Two: Shoppers' Rights

Know your consumer rights, © Saga, *Online shoppers 'unaware of consumer rights',* © Guardian News and Media Ltd 2010, *Don't keep me hanging on a customer service line,* © Which?, *OFT warning on misleading pricing practices,* © Office of Fair Trading, *Are consumers turning away from credit?,* © Moneyfacts, *Consumers deserve more credit, says Which?,* © Which?, *Identity fraud and identity theft,* © Action Fraud, *Fraud costs the UK over £38 billion, says the National Fraud Authority,* © Crown copyright is reproduced with the permission of Her Majesty's Stationery Office.

Chapter Three: Ethical Buying

Ethical consumerism, how we got here, © Ethical Consumer Research Association, *How to harness ethical shopping's 'floating voters',* © Ethical Trading Initiative, *Life without supermarkets: escaping choice overload,* © The Ecologist, *Shoppers: put your money where your mouth is,* © Guardian News and Media Ltd, *Retail myths,* © British Retail Consortium, *Ethical labels add millions to cost of food,* © Telegraph Group Limited, London 2010, *Purely extravagant,* © YouGov, *UK consumers fail to follow through on their support for Corporate Social Responsibility,* © YouGov, *The big names behind your food brands,* © Which?, *Fairtrade FAQ,* © Fairtrade Foundation, *New research finds Fair Trade movement is a distraction, not a solution,* © Institute of Economic Affairs, *Retail ethics and green retailing 2011: more than plastic bags?,* © Centre for Retail Research, *Children and advertising,* © Advertising Standards Authority, *The impact of the commercial world on children's wellbeing,* © Crown copyright is reproduced with the permission of Her Majesty's Stationery Office, *The commercialisation of childhood,* © Loughborough University.

Illustrations

Pages 6, 15, 20, 35: Don Hatcher; pages 8, 17, 28, 37: Angelo Madrid; pages 12, 23: Bev Aisbett; pages 14, 16, 29, 38: Simon Kneebone.

Cover photography

Left: © pipp. Centre: © Lotus Head. Right: © Kat Jackson.

Additional acknowledgements

And with thanks to the Independence team: Mary Chapman, Sandra Dennis and Jan Sunderland.

Lisa Firth
Cambridge
April, 2011

ASSIGNMENTS

The following tasks aim to help you think through the issues surrounding consumer rights and ethics and provide a better understanding of the topic.

1 Read *The problem isn't consumption – it's Consumerism* on page 2. Do you think this article makes a valid point? Write a short summary of the arguments presented, including clear definitions of consumption and consumerism and stating how far you agree with the writer.

2 Watch the film 'Minority Report' starring Tom Cruise. In this vision of the future, omnipresent animated billboards which can recognise individuals via an iris scan are able to advertise directly to them. Write a review of the film, focusing on what it has to say about our potential future as consumers. If you wish to take this activity further, you could go on to write your own short story about a futuristic society in which consumerism is central to citizens' way of life. Would it be a utopia or dystopia?

3 Over the course of a fortnight, keep a shopper's diary, logging every time you make a purchase, what you buy and how much money you spend. At the end of this time, review your diary. What do you buy most regularly? Are you spending within your means? Were all your purchases planned, or were some impulse buys?

4 Watch a commercial television channel at a time when children's programmes are most commonly scheduled, for example immediately after school or on a Saturday morning. Keep a record of all the advertisements that are shown, making a note of the product advertised and the techniques used to make it appealing to children. Are the advertisers behaving responsibly? Would you say that childhood is becoming increasingly commercialised?

5 Read *Consumers see little difference between national and store brands* on page 11. Create a survey to find out what brands people buy and use it to take a poll of your class. You could focus on one type of product, for example breakfast cereals, or give your questions a wider focus. Analyse your results: do most people buy national brands (such as Kellogg's) or supermarkets' own brands?

6 Create an illustrated booklet aimed at young people, designed to inform them of their rights as consumers.

7 Read articles from *Chapter 3: Ethical Buying*. What are the main issues which a would-be ethical shopper needs to be aware of? Make a list.

8 'Ethical consumerism is all very well for the affluent. I would love to buy only locally-sourced, free-range organic food for my family but I just can't afford it, especially in a recession.' Are you sympathetic to this view? Is there any way to shop ethically on a budget?

9 'The Fair Trade movement is a distraction from the problem of unfair trade practices, not a solution.' Read the articles on pages 32-33 and carry out your own research before debating this statement in two groups, with one arguing in favour and the other against.

10 Were you aware of the big names behind some ethical brands, revealed in the article on page 31? Does this bother you? Would it cause you to alter your buying habits? Discuss your feelings with a partner.

11 Look at the history of consumerism, starting in the 1920s with the emergence of mass production. How has the increasing availability and affordability of goods changed the way in which we live and work? Has the emergence of new technologies like television and the Internet made a difference to how we consume? Create a timeline showing the major developments.

12 Read the book 'Confessions of a Shopaholic' by Sophie Kinsella. Do you think this book reinforces or trivialises the problems faced by those who compulsively spend and those close to them? Write a review.

13 Do some research into The People's Supermarket, which states that its vision is 'to create a commercially sustainable, social enterprise that achieves its growth and profitability targets whilst operating within values based on community development and cohesion.' Do you think this is a valuable initiative? Write a summary of the supermarket's background and aims.

14 What makes an effective advertisement? Think of ads you have found memorable or persuasive and the reasons you think they worked.